Metal Detecting

A Beginner's Guide to
Mastering the Greatest Hobby In the World

By Mark Smith

D1014308

Metal Detecting

ISBN-13: 978-1494964412
ISBN-10: 1494964414
Metal Detecting: A Beginner's Guide to the Greatest Hobby in the World

Table of Contents

Metal Detecting

Introduction

There is something really incredible about removing a chunk of earth and seeing a glimmer of metal encrusted in the soil. Your mind races as you reach down to pluck your new found treasure from its prison of dirt. What could it be? The possibilities are limitless.

Your heart starts to beat a little faster as you realize that you have just unearthed a piece of treasure that may have not seen the light of day for hundreds of years. With hands that have now become a little unsteady, you try to brush away some of the clinging dirt to get a better look at your find.

Could it be a lost relic from hundreds or thousands of years ago? Could it be an old coin made from copper, bronze, silver or even gold? Could it be a piece of jewelry packed

Introduction

full of precious stones? Could it be a piece of history from a historical battle where lives were put on the line? It could be any of these things and more!

What you now hold in your hands is a piece of history. It may be worth a lot of money, but the real value is the history that you have just brought to light. Think of who may have held or used this piece of treasure. Think of the places it has been. Think of the lives it has changed. If it could talk, think of the story that it could tell you.

This is the reality of what can only be described as the greatest hobby in the world, metal detecting. Yeah I said it, and I think it is 100% true. Metal detecting is the greatest hobby in the world, and anyone can do it!

There is a world of treasure buried right beneath our feet, and it is just waiting for you or me to dig it up. There are people who are digging up buried treasure right now as you read these words. This is not some made up BS story. There are people winning the metal detecting lottery every minute of every single day. I have done it more times than I can count. Are you ready to go claim your share of treasure and history?

My First Time Metal Detecting

I remember the very first time I used a metal detector. It wasn't even mine. I purchased one for my five year old son. He always loved to find things, so I thought a metal detector would make a great Christmas present.

The night before Christmas my wife and I decided to take about $5.00 in change and hide it all over the front yard. I even went so far as to make a little treasure map to help my son find everything that we had buried the night before.

The next morning came way too early like Christmas morning always does. My son tore through his presents really quick. The metal detector was the last one he opened. He had no idea what it was.

I explained it to him and from the moment I said, "treasure" a light grew in his eyes. Then he saw the "authentic" treasure map and his jaw dropped. He could not get the batteries in the metal detector quick enough. His little fingers fumbled with excitement and anticipation.

I quickly explained how the detector worked. There was nothing fancy about it. You turned it on and it beeped when it moved over metal. My son went to work using his treasure map and the metal detector.

My First Time Metal Detecting

His new metal detector quickly located a target that was not on the treasure map. I was a little confused because I did nut bury anything in this spot. He dug up a nail. He got another signal that was not on the treasure map. He dug up my lost pair of pliers. So that is where they went. He was laughing and having a good time.

My son was finding stuff everywhere in our front yard. He was also finding coins all over the place. He quickly had a couple of dollars in modern coins. Then he pulled an antique silver ring from the front yard. That is when it hit me. Wow, metal detectors really do work. I looked at my wife who just rolled her eyes and said, "Oh boy."

My wife already new that I wanted to go out to the store and buy the most expensive metal detector that I could find, but she was wrong. This was one hobby that I was going to step lightly into.

I was in the same exact situation where you might find yourself right this minute. I knew that I wanted a metal detector, but I had no idea where I should begin. I had a mild case of treasure fever. I wanted to see what else I could dig up. I started thinking about old coins and lost treasures. I never once considered finding lost jewelry.

That was several years ago. I have owned over a dozen different metal detectors over the years. Some have worked better than others, but one thing is for certain, I love digging up treasure. I never seemed to get tired of finding coins, relics, jewelry and gold.

Before I started metal detecting, I was an avid fisherman. That was about to change. Metal detecting quickly became my priority hobby, and I let the dust collect on all of my fishing gear. I was finding all sorts of treasures and my hobby was paying for itself. I had created a monster.

HA HA HA! IT'S ALIVE!

It was not long before I stepped neck deep into metal detecting and purchased an expensive machine with all the bells and whistles. This improved my finds dramatically, and I have been happily digging up lost treasure every chance I get.

I quickly learned that using a metal detector is a lot like everything else in life. You will have to dig through some trash before you find the real treasure below.

Why Do You Want to Start Metal Detecting?

This is kind of a silly question, but it is very important to have an answer to this question before you start your life long addiction to treasure hunting. Once the treasure bug bites you, it can be really difficult to shake it. Your significant other may even get upset with you because you are spending all of your free time hunting for treasure. Just make sure to bring home all the jewelry you dig up and everything should be fine.

We all want to start metal detecting for the same reason. We want to find buried treasure. This treasure could be old relics, old coins, modern coins, lost jewelry or lost caches. If you put a little bit of time and effort into metal detecting, you will be able to find all of this and more, but knowing why you want to start metal detecting will help you determine what type of metal detector is best for you.

There are hundreds of different metal detectors on the market today. Choosing which one is right for you is probably the most complicated thing about metal detecting. There are machines that are made for specific purposes.

For instance, if your interest is to find older coins, then you would be better off with a machine that was designed for coin shooting. If you want to find gold nuggets, then you are better off with a machine that was designed for finding gold nuggets. If you want to find a clown, then you should stop reading this book and go to the circus. I hope you get my point. There are metal detectors for just about every type of metal and style of metal detecting. Owning the right machine makes a world of difference.

You may be saying to yourself, "I want to be able to find everything. I want to find old coins, lost jewelry, relics, and gold nuggets." We all want to be able to find everything, and luckily there are machines on the market that are multi-purpose. These machines have been designed to help you locate all sorts of treasure, and most of them work as advertised.

The main thing to remember is this. Your new hobby is supposed to be fun. Don't over complicate things by getting a machine that has a huge learning curve. You will quickly lose interest. The more time that you have to spend learning how to use a metal detector, the less time you will be able to spend digging up buried treasures.

If you don't already own the machine, my advice to you would be to start simple. Work your way towards a more expensive machine with all the bells and whistles. Get a taste for what metal detecting is really about before you start spending a lot of money on something that is going to collect dust. You may quickly find out that you don't really like digging up pull tabs and all the other garbage that you have to dig up to get to the good targets.

Why Do You Want to Start Metal Detecting?

As of this writing, metal detectors have come a long way, but many of them still can't determine some of the most common trash from some of the most sought after buried treasures. They are getting close, but they are not quite there yet.

Digging up trash is just part of the metal detecting game. You can use your machine to help you ignore the trash, but you could be passing up potentially good targets. I will talk about this more later on.

For every piece of garbage you dig up, you are one step closer to finding some very valuable buried treasure. I didn't believe that I could find a single item that would pay for my most expensive metal detector, but I have. I have done this on several occasions actually, and it is an amazing feeling when you dig up an extremely valuable treasure.

In many ways valuable treasure is a lot like trash. What I consider to be a valuable treasure, other people might consider to be junk. I often get asked, "Have you found any treasure with that machine?" My reply is always the same. "Well that depends on what you consider to be treasure." You might find more value in an old World War II relic than a gold ring. Value is relative.

Learning the Lingo

Everything seems to have its own lingo, and metal detecting is no different. I will be using quite a few terms in this book that you might not be familiar with. I might have already done this. (sorry about that) Before we can dive in and start digging up treasure, it might be a good idea to learn the lingo. This will allow you to walk the walk and talk the talk. Can you dig it?

You can skip this part if you already consider yourself to be a metal detecting linguistics major, but if you think **canslaw** is a canned form of coleslaw, then you might want to keep reading. Knowledge is power they say.

Air test
This is something a lot of people will do the moment they get their first machine. They may set the machine up on a table and start waving metal objects in front of the coil. Other people will try and determine how well a metal detector works by doing the same thing. This is called performing an air test. You just wave a metal object through the air in front of the coil.

This is not a good indication of how well a metal detector will work. Everything changes once an item has been buried in the ground. **See Halo Effect below**.

All metal

Learning the Lingo

Most modern metal detectors have some sort of discrimination capabilities. This allows you to filter out some of the junk metal targets. All Metal is hunting with no discrimination at all. Your metal detector will alert you to any type of metal under the coil.

Black sand

Black sand can be a great sign that you are really close to gold, but it can wreak havoc on some metal detectors. The black sand is not sand at all. It is actually very small pieces of iron oxide or magnetite.

This is also known as heavily mineralized ground. You may need to make adjustments to your metal detector in order for it to function properly in high ground mineralization, and some machines may not even work at all.

Bling

It is always great finding bling. Bling is any form of jewelry that is made from precious metals, but the best bling is jewelry that is loaded with precious stones. Bling can make your heart skip a beat!

Cache

This is something that every metal detecting enthusiast dreams about. A cache is a hoard of valuables that have been hidden. The cache could consist of hundreds of old coins, or a collection of items. Finding a cache can be like winning the metal detecting lottery!

Canslaw

Grab a big bowl and a fork and get ready for dinner! Canslaw is on the menu tonight. Canslaw is small pieces of aluminum cans that get magically scattered around your favorite hunting grounds. It is almost as if someone scattered these little pieces everywhere just to make you work a little harder for your treasure. Could it be the canslaw fairy?

Have you ever seen a lawnmower run over an aluminum can? It makes canslaw. Dredging equipment also makes canslaw. You will learn to dislike canslaw very much.

Clad

Clad is another thing that you will just have to get used to because you are going to be finding a lot of it. Clad is any modern money that is made from non-precious metals. At least you can spend this stuff, and its better than filling your finds pouch with canslaw!

Coil

The round part at the end of the metal detector. It is also called the loop in certain parts of the world.

Coin ball

Coin balls are always great. They are small round chunks of earth with a coin inside. Kind of like candy, but much better and healthier for you too.

Learning the Lingo

Coin shooting

Target practice is a great way to ensure that your aim is always spot on. Most people prefer cans, bottles and paper targets. Coin shooting is when you practice your aim on small coins. I am just pulling your leg here. I wanted to see if you were still paying attention.

Coin shooting is the art of using a metal detector to locate nothing but old valuable coins. It can be a very addictive form of metal detecting, especially when you start pulling old silver coins out of the ground. Once you pull a gold coin out of the ground, your life will never be the same again.

Coin spill aka pocket spill

This is when the entire contents of someone's pockets are spilled resulting in multiple coins in one very small area.

Cut

This is a term that you will hear when people are talking about metal detecting on the beach. This is when a large portion of sand has been removed from the beach. It looks as if the entire beach was cut with a large knife.

Digger

The tool that you use to dig up your treasure. Owning a metal detector is not enough. You will also need some accessories to help you retrieve your treasure.

Discrimination (Disc for short)

There are some metal detectors that have the ability to tell the user what type of metal their piece of treasure is made from before they even dig it up. By using this information, it can be easy to ignore metal objects that are most likely trash.

If you are new to metal detecting, then you will be very surprised by the amount of trash that is buried right under the surface of the ground. Sometimes there is so much trash that it makes it almost impossible to locate the good targets among all the trash. This is when discrimination comes in really handy.

There is also a downside to using too much discrimination. You could be missing out on some very valuable targets. If you discriminate aluminum pull tabs and foil, you will also be discriminating fine gold. Always use your best judgment when using discrimination with your metal detector.

Electrolysis
Using electricity to create a chemical reaction. In this case, people use electrolysis to help them clean pieces of treasure without causing any sort of significant damage to the treasure.

False or falsing
When a metal detector gives an indication of buried treasure when there is really nothing there. It is giving you false signals. There are all sorts of things that can do this.

Learning the Lingo

The most common is user error.

Swinging a coil too fast, or in an erratic pattern will always cause false signals. Bumping your coil against the ground or anything else for that matter can cause your metal detector to give false signals.

Electromagnetic interference can also cause false signals. Cell phones, cordless phones, routers, power lines, and electric dog fences are the most common cause of this problem. Highly mineralized ground can also cause false signals.

Ferrous targets
Any buried or recovered piece of treasure that contains iron. You are most likely looking for non-ferrous targets like: gold, silver, platinum or palladium. You get the picture.

Don't automatically assume that an iron target is trash. There are plenty of great relics out there that are made from iron and there could be good targets being masked by the iron targets. **See Iron Masking below for more details**.

Finds
Anything you find with your metal detector!

Finds pouch
The place where you store all your finds while you are

metal detecting.

Grid or gridding
The term "gridding an area" comes from a method that archaeologists use to recover historical items. When an archaeologist makes a good discovery, they will immediately make a grid of the area using markers and string. This breaks down one large area into several smaller areas. Each smaller area is then meticulously searched.

This same concept can be applied to metal detecting what may be considered a really good spot, but without the markers. It is easy enough to go very slow in a very tight, very specific pattern that ensures not one inch or centimeter of ground is missed.

Ground balance
Some areas will have more minerals in the ground than others. Ground balancing your metal detector is the process of adjusting your metal detector to the minerals in the ground at your current location. There are metal detectors that do this automatically, and there are some that require you to do a manual ground balance.

Halo effect
Metal items that have been buried for extended periods of time create what is called a halo effect. These metal items create an ionization field or halo that amplifies the target. The halo effect can be very obvious for older buried coins.

You may get a very strong signal with your metal detector, but as you start removing earth, the signal gets fainter and sometimes it will even completely disappear. You may even think you had a false signal. If you keep digging, you will find that the piece of treasure is still in the hole.

When you removed the earth, you also broke the ionization halo and now your metal detector can't "see" the buried treasure. That is where using a really good pinpointer comes in. Don't know what a pinpointer is? Don't worry, it's in this list too.

This entire concept is up for debate. Some people say it does happen and some say it does not. I have seen it happen myself on several occasions. I talk a little more about this concept in the chapter titled: Recovery Part 2.

Hammered site
This is an area where everyone and their entire family have already spent a good amount of time metal detecting. The chances of finding really good treasure are slim, but there is always a possibility that everyone else may have already missed a thing or two.

High tones
A high pitched tone that a metal detector makes when locating certain targets. With a lot of metal detectors, this means silver!

Learning the Lingo

Hot rock
I really don't care for hot rocks. Hot rocks are rocks that have metallic properties. To your metal detector, these rocks look like a piece of treasure. Some metal detectors will allow you to discriminate out hot rocks, but remember using too much discrimination will often mean you are leaving behind some good stuff.

Keeper
Anything you find while metal detecting that you keep. Gold and silver would be keepers. Cans and rusty iron are not, unless of course they are relics.

Low tones
The exact opposite of high tones. On some machines, low tones mean you have hit the mother lode. It could be gold, platinum or a crummy old pull tab.

Iron masking
Masking is not good. Masking happens when iron is in close proximity to a good piece of treasure. The iron effectively masks the good target. Your metal detector only responds to the iron. Nine times out of ten, the good target is ignored.

But there are metal detectors that can still locate good pieces of treasure even if they are right on top of or underneath smaller pieces of iron. With these metal detectors, masking is less noticeable! Hooray! Gold for everyone who is lucky enough to own a metal detector like this.

I have and still do find plenty of great pieces of treasure that are buried right underneath huge chunks of iron without ever knowing they were there. If the iron is really big, your metal detector will not be able to see the treasure underneath it. At least not with current metal detectors on the market today.

I made a rule for myself. If at anytime I am detecting and I locate an iron target that is bigger than a nail, (I can usually tell how big a target is with my machine.) I dig it up. Who knows what it could be, and who knows what could be underneath or even in it.

I was hunting an area not too long ago that was loaded with civil war relics. My metal detector alerted me to a big iron target. My mind wandered, and I thought it could be a gun or a sword. I quickly started uncovering the target. It was not a gun or a sword. It was an old chunk of pipe.

I was a little disappointed in my find, but that pipe was not the only thing buried in that spot. Right under the iron pipe, I uncovered several civil war bullets and other relics that were being masked by the iron pipe.

Notch
Notching is using a form of discrimination to accurately identify only certain types of metal. Notch is also the nickname of the guy that created the video game called

Minecraft.

Nulling or null signal
Some metal detector brands create a constant sound. This constant sound is called a threshold. When the threshold sound stops or completely disappears, it nulls. This is usually the result of a large piece of iron. This is the perfect example of masking. Any good targets are masked by the null or lack of sound the metal detector makes.

Pinpointer
A small hand held metal detector that you use to pinpoint the exact location of a buried piece of treasure once you have removed a big old chunk of earth. I will go over using a pinpointer a little later in the recovery section of this book.

Pinpointing
Using a metal detector or a pinpointer to determine the exact location of a buried piece of treasure.

Plug
When you are metal detecting an area of nice land, you always want to cut a plug. Cutting a plug is the art (yes cutting a good plug is an art form) of using a digging tool to remove a plug of soil in order to get to the piece of treasure buried below it.

A good plug will go right back in the ground, and no one will ever be able to tell that you were even there. Unless the plug you just created was on top of a chimpmunk's burrow. Then you might have one angry chipmunk!

I will go over cutting a good plug a little bit later in the recovery section of this book.

Pounded site
Same as hammered site.

PI or Pulse Induction
This is a type of metal detector that reacts to all metals. They are known to go very deep and they are not affected by highly mineralized ground. They can see ferrous and non-ferrous metals right through any type of mineralization. They are great machines. Every serious metal detector enthusiast should own at least one.

Pull tab
Get used to seeing this little guy because there is really good chance you will be digging up quite a few of them when you start searching for treasure. This is the part of a aluminum can that you use to open the can. It can be the type that you actually pull off to open the can, or it can be the small piece that you use to open the can. Pull tabs..... Ugh

Probe
A small tool that is used to help you locate a coin buried in the ground. It looks very similar to an icepick or a screw driver. Using a probe to locate a coin buried in the ground

can be difficult, but it is the preferred method of recovery when you don't want to disturb the grass. It creates a very small hole that is virtually unnoticeable. I will go over using a probe a little later in the recovery section of this book.

Relics
Buried pieces of history that may not have monetary value based on the metals they are made from. Relics still hold a significant place in history giving them a historical value.

Repeatable signal
Before you start digging, you always want to make sure that you get a good repeatable signal. When items are buried really deep, or when a coin is laying on its side, you may need to swing your coil over the target from different angles in order to get a good repeatable signal. This refers to the audio or visual indication that your metal detector is giving you. If the signal is repeatable, then start digging!

Ring or rang up
How a piece of treasure shows up on your metal detector with either a visual or audio signal, or both.

Sensitivity
A setting that allows you to really crank up the power of your metal detector. A higher sensitivity means your metal detector will locate targets deeper, but it will also mean there is a greater chance of it falsing. The goal is to locate the perfect sensitivity setting that recovers deep targets

without producing false signals.

Signal
The audio or visual clue your metal detector gives you indicating there is a metal object buried under the coil.

Sweep
The distance your coil moves from left to right, or right to left if you are a lefty.

Target
The piece of treasure that you are trying to recover. Targets are a really good thing!

Target ID
Some metal detectors will use a visual indicator to help you determine what your target is before you even start digging it up. This is the target ID. It could be a numerical value, or it could be a visual on-screen meter.

Target separation
Some of the more expensive metal detectors on the market today use a high tech feature called target separation. This allows the metal detector to respond to more than one target in a very small area. Target separation can be a very good thing once you learn how to effectively use it.

Test garden
An area where people plant items to test the efficiency of their metal detector. While this sounds like a good idea, it

can not give you a 100% accurate representation of the capabilities of your metal detector. See Halo Effect above.

Threshold
The constant hum that some metal detectors make when in use. The threshold changes when a target is under the coil.

Tone ID
The audio signal that comes from your metal detector. The specific tone can help you identify the target before you even think about digging it up.

Tot Lot
This can be a really good place to hunt. Tot lot is another word for playground.

Troy Ounce
A unit of measurement that is used to measure the mass of precious metals.

Visual ID
Some metal detectors feature a small screen where visual clues will help you determine what might be buried beneath your feet. These are visual IDs.

Whatzit
There is a really good chance you will find plenty of these. These are pieces of metal that can't be identified. This does not mean that you should toss them in the trash. Just because you don't know what it is doesn't mean someone

else won't know. You could have something very valuable. I will show you how to identify things you can't identify a little later.

Congratulations! You are now a metal detecting linguistics expert. There are some other metal detecting terms that are directly related to specific types of coins, but since this publication is world wide, I decided not to include them.

A Closer Look at the Metal Detector

To say that all metal detectors are created the same would be a lie. Each and every metal detector brand and model are completely different. They all serve the same purpose though, and for the most part they all have the same basic parts. Almost every single metal detector can easily be broken down into six distinct pieces. It will help you to have a firm understanding of what these six pieces are and how they help you find treasure. Take a closer look at this diagram.

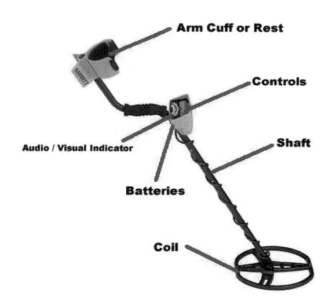

A Closer Look at the Metal Detector

These are the six distinct pieces that almost each and every metal detector has, and to make things even more confusing, you will find that just about every distinct piece on every metal detector is a little bit different. Here is an explanation of what each distinct piece is. Let's start at the top and work our way down.

The Arm Cuff or Arm Rest
This is one area of the metal detector that is always overlooked. Most people get so excited about the possibilities of finding treasure that they are only worried about how deep a detector will detect, or how well it will discriminate trash from treasure.

These two features are very important, but you will not be able to find any amount of treasure if your arm is sore from swinging your metal detector. This is why it is very important to pay close attention to the arm cuff. The arm cuff should be comfortable like your favorite pair of old shoes, socks or underwear. Okay, I admit. I may have gone too far there, but you get the point.

The importance of a comfortable arm cuff is paramount. This is the one area of your metal detector that gets the most resistance from your body. I know this for a fact because on one of my metal detectors, the arm cuff broke during a big hunt. I thought to myself, "No big deal. I can keep swinging." Boy was I wrong. I never realized just how important this little arm cuff was. I could not swing my detector for more than five minutes without it.

A Closer Look at the Metal Detector

Lightweight metal detectors won't be a problem, but this was a large waterproof machine.

This brings me to the next point about the arm cuff. It needs to be durable. This is one piece that I have managed to break on almost all of my "heavy duty" detectors. If you can take a metal detector for a test drive, pay very close attention to the comfort and durability of the arm cuff. It really makes a huge difference.

Almost all arm cuffs will have some sort of strap that will keep your arm in place. Arm cuffs are also usually lined with some type of thin soft foam as well. Both of these are very important. Without the strap, it becomes very difficult to use your metal detector for any extended period of time. The same goes for the foam lining.

Quick Tip!
I already mentioned that there was a time when the arm cuff broke on my favorite metal detector. It was going to be a few weeks before I could get a replacement, and there was no way that I was going to wait two weeks to start hunting again. It was the middle of metal detecting season. Yes there is a season for metal detecting. It is hard to metal detect in the snow, so any season when it is not snowing is metal detecting season. Here is what I did to fix the problem.

I went out to my local home improvement store and purchased some PVC pipe. I got a piece that was about 4-5 inches in diameter. I went ahead and bought a few feet of it.

When I got home, I cut off about a 6 inch section of pipe. I then cut the pipe in half. I cut it so that I now had a piece of pipe that was about six inches long and shaped like a "U."

This would become my temporary arm rest. I covered the rough edges with tape, and used a velcro strap that I purchased a few weeks earlier at a garage sale. I drilled two small holes in my makeshift arm rest and attached it to the shaft of my metal detector. This was two years ago. I still use this arm cuff to this date!

A Closer Look at the Metal Detector

That's a picture of my homemade arm cuff. Crude, but it got the job done!

The Controls

This is the next part on the machine, and it can be the most difficult part to figure out if you have a really fancy machine. The controls will always vary depending on the machine you have. I can't really go into too much detail about what the different controls are, but I can tell you that the more time you spend with your metal detector the better you will be at using it.

Read the manual, and then play with your machine for a little while. Then read the manual again. The more time you put into the machine, the more you will understand what it is trying to tell you.

Audio / Visual Indicators

These will also vary greatly depending on the machine that you have purchased. One of my favorite machines has no visual indicator at all. It has an excellent pair of headphones that tell me everything I need to know. That brings me to my next point.

I would always recommend using headphones with your metal detector. If your machine does not have them, then there is not much you can do about it, but headphones can really make a huge difference. They will block out all of the background noise that may make you miss some of the more faint sounds. Make sure that the headphones you get are comfortable. You will be wearing them for a long time.

As far as the visual indicators go, they can be simple target indicators, or they can be advanced touch screens that will tell you what the target is, how deep it is buried and your exact coordinates.

You can easily spend too much money on a metal detector. I tell everyone the same thing. Pick out a machine that is not too expensive if you are just starting out. It may turn out that you don't even like metal detecting, and it would be a shame to spend a lot of money on a metal detector that is just going to collect dust in your closet. Start out small, and when you get hooked, upgrade to a better machine.

Batteries

Unless some new type of power source has been discovered since the time that I wrote this book, then batteries are going to be one of the most important parts to your new metal detector. Without good batteries, you will not be finding anything at all. Always make sure you have fresh batteries, and it never hurts to have a nice spare set too.

Most modern machines will have some sort of rechargeable battery pack. Make sure that you have a spare pack because rechargeable batteries are not always the most reliable, and you would be very angry with yourself if your battery pack died right during the middle of the hunt of a lifetime!

A Closer Look at the Metal Detector

The Shaft
This is the long portion of the metal detector that goes
from the controls down to the coil. The coil is usually
attached to the shaft. There are some machines where the
shaft is adjustable. The longer the shaft is, the more ground
you will be able to cover. A longer shaft may also be more
difficult to swing for long periods of time.

I even went so far as to replace the entire length of the
stock shaft that came with one of my metal detectors with
a longer piece of lightweight aluminum pipe. By extending
the length of the shaft on my metal detector, it gave me
about two feet of more coverage when I swing from left to
right.

More coverage means more chances to locate some
treasure. You will learn over time that metal detecting is a
very precise hobby. The more ground you cover, the better
your chances are of recovering some great treasure. This
by no means is an indicator that you should try to complete
any sort of speed runs. Slow and steady wins the race with
this concept.

The Coil
There seems to be some argument in this area of the metal
detector. There are some people that think a large coil is
the best way to recover more treasure, and there are some
people who think that a smaller coil is the only way to go.
I have used both and here is where I weigh in on the

subject. There is a right time and a wrong time to use each one.

I got excited and purchased an aftermarket coil for my favorite machine. It did allow me to cover more ground which meant that I could possibly find more treasure. It was also harder to pinpoint, it did not locate targets as deep as the stock coil did and at times it got in the way. I tried it for a few months, and ended up going back to my stock coil.

There are also times when a smaller coil is the best choice. It will allow you to easily detect in some very small tight spaces. Just imagine trying to use a metal detector that has a coil that is 14 inches (35 centimeters) in diameter in an area of woods where the trees are about 10 inches (25 centimeters) apart.

Do you think that would work? No it would not. The person that is using a smaller 8 or 6 inch coil (20 or 15 centimeter coil) will be able to walk right into the woods and locate all of the treasure while the person with the large coil is trying to figure out how to get their metal detector into the woods.

A smaller coil will also make it much easier to locate good targets in an area where there are a lot of trashy targets. With most small coils, you sacrifice depth. There is a time and a place for everything.

A Closer Look at the Metal Detector

Quick Tip!

In order to get the best results from your metal detector, you should keep your coil as close to the ground as possible at all times. People have a tendency to lift the coil up as they get to the end of their swings. This will cause the machine to false, and it will also cause it to lose sensitivity. It takes a little bit of practice to keep the coil level the entire time you are using it but it really makes a huge difference.

Remember, part of the joy of metal detecting is slowing down and checking out everything around you. Let the machine tell you where the targets are with its audio responses while your eyes scan the ground ahead of you. This is also a good practice that will keep you from stepping in poop, traps or on a nasty snake. Keep your ears focused on the sound and your eyes focused on the ground in front of you.

Metal Detector Brands

Competition among manufacturers is good for consumers. It gives us plenty of great choices. You will find that there are a handful of metal detector manufacturers out there, and the prices range quite dramatically from manufacturer to manufacturer.

Which metal detector brand is the best?
The best metal detector brand is the one that works for you. Pure and simple. You could buy a top of the line metal detector with all the latest and greatest technological advancements and still get out hunted by someone that really knows how to use a machine that costs a quarter of what you paid. It all boils down to how well you know how to use that machine to locate treasure, not the price, model or manufacturer.

Some people get really bent out of shape when you say one metal detector brand is better than another. I guess they feel insulted. That is not what this next section is all about. This next section is simply to inform you about all of the great metal detector brand choices out there. I have and still do own quite a few of these brands, and I will be sharing my personal experiences and knowledge about them. These experiences in no way mean that one machine is better than the other.

Here is an alphabetical list of the most common metal

detector brands as of this writing.

Bounty Hunter Metal Detectors

The first land metal detector that I purchased for myself was a Bounty Hunter. It worked perfectly, and it was enough to get me hooked. Bounty Hunter machines are an excellent entry point into the great hobby of metal detecting, but why?

Most Bounty Hunter metal detectors come with a very affordable price tag. The low price tag can be all it takes to convince someone to buy. It is the number one reason I bought mine, but Bounty Hunter machines are also effective, lightweight and relatively easy to use.

Will they find buried treasure?

Yes they will. They may not have the greatest depth or discrimination, but Bounty Hunter machines are worth every single penny as long as you get out there and use them. I paid for mine within two months of detecting tot lots. All of those coins add up really quick.

Who would benefit the most with a Bounty Hunter metal detector?

Bounty Hunters are great for anyone who is just starting out in the hobby. Children will love them, and their lower price tag makes them an excellent gift idea. Their simplicity also makes them a great choice for someone who doesn't do well with technology. There are some models that are more advanced than others. The more advanced models do come with a learning curve. Overall these are great entry level machines.

Detector Pro Metal Detectors

Feel like getting your feet wet? Do you want to search salt and freshwater beaches for buried pirate treasures? If you are planning on doing some water hunting, but you don't want to spend a lot of money on an expensive waterproof metal detector, then a Detector Pro metal detector might be the right choice for you. They are a lower priced entry level water hunting machine.

Metal detecting in the water is a completely different thing, and metal detecting the beach is entirely different as well. The unique thing about this line of metal detectors is the fact that the controls are all within the headphones. This leaves nothing but a shaft and coil to swing in the water.

Believe me when I say that metal detecting in the water can really tire you out. I have done it for years. You may be able to swing a metal detector all day long on dry land, but as soon as you submerge it, you have to deal with the resistance of the water. Having all of the controls mounted on the shaft makes it even more difficult to swing for extended periods of time. Your arm can and will get tired much quicker.

The Detector Pro line of metal detectors lightens the load by keeping the controls in the headphones. This makes it easier to use these machines for extended periods of time while in the water.

Will Detector Pro metal detectors find treasure?
They will find plenty of treasure as long as you put some time into water hunting. Who knows, maybe you will find some lost Spanish gold or silver. It happens more often than you may think. I may have even found a piece or eight.

Who would benefit the most with a Detector Pro metal detector?
Detector pro machines are great entry level water hunting machines. If you have the desire to get wet and find treasure, then this may be the machine for you.

Official Company Website:
http://www.detectorpro.com/

Fisher or Fisher Lab Metal Detectors

There is something that can be said about Fisher metal detectors that simply can't be said about any other metal detector manufacturer. Fisher metal detectors were the first metal detectors in existence. They got their start in a garage lab in California way back in 1931and believe it or not the very first metal detector was born from an accident.

Fisher Labs was manufacturing aircraft navigation tools. Airline pilots noticed that these navigation tools would create errors in bearings when close to metal objects, or if they were used in certain areas of highly mineralized ground. These errors gave birth to the Metallascope. The world's very first metal detector, and the rest is history!

Fast forward to today and you will find Fisher Labs is cranking out some of the best metal detectors on the market. Fisher currently manufactures several very affordable entry level machines, as well as some pretty sophisticated ones too. You can find a simple entry level machine, all purpose machines, machines designed just for coins, machines designed just for gold and machines designed for relics.

Will Fisher Labs metal detectors find treasure?
You can't go wrong with a Fisher. These machines will find plenty of treasure as long as you put in the time. Fisher Labs has every type of metal detecting covered with their

extensive product line.

Who will benefit the most with a Fisher Labs metal detector?

Being that Fisher Labs have just about everything covered, these machines are great for anyone from the first timer to the hardcore metal detecting enthusiast. The entry level machines are simple and lightweight and they find treasure. The more advanced machines are the perfect fit for someone who knows exactly what they are looking for.

Official company website:

http://www.fisherlab.com/

Garrett Metal Detectors

Garrett makes some of the best metal detectors on the market. If you are new to the hobby, then Garrett has a machine for you. If you are a seasoned pro, then Garrett has got you covered as well. If you want a machine designed to find gold, then you are covered. If you want a machine that finds relics deep, Garrett has one. They have every type of metal detecting scenario covered.

I have and still own a couple of Garrett machines, and they have never let me down. 9 out of 10 metal detecting enthusiasts have and still use the infamous Garrett Pro Pinpointer, me included. These are just a few reasons why Garrett metal detectors are so popular.

The entry level Garrett metal detectors are very affordable, and they are simple to use. Garrett is also known for creating machines that are tough and reliable as well.

Will Garrett metal detectors find treasure?
You don't get to be one of the most popular metal detector manufacturers in the entire world by producing a product that doesn't work. There are plenty of people who have found great pieces of treasure with entry level Garrett machines. It happens more often than you may think. Garrett metal detectors will find plenty of great treasure.

Who will benefit the most with a Garrett metal

detector?

Anyone who has the desire to go out and find treasure. The entry level models are great for kids or people who just want to get a feel for the hobby, and the more advanced models are perfect for people who have already spent a good amount of time swinging a coil. Garrett has the market fully covered.

Official company website:

http://www.garrett.com/

Minelab Metal Detectors

Minelab metal detectors have some serious advantages. Minelab is a world wide company. They have locations all over the world, and their metal detectors are some of the best on the market. I currently own two Minelab machines and I take them with me just about every where I go. You just never know when a good metal detecting opportunity will make itself known. I am always prepared.

Minelab manufactures a metal detector for every purpose. They have specialty machines that will locate gold in highly mineralized ground conditions. They have machines that will see through iron trash and reveal gold and silver below. They have machines that are multi-purpose, and they have machines that can be used deep below the surface of the ocean. Minelab machines are favored by beach hunters all over the globe. Minelab metal detectors work, and they work very well. It isjust that simple. Some of their products simply can't be beat.

You will pay a higher price tag for most Minelab metal detectors, but they are worth every penny. All it takes is one small piece of treasure to pay for your metal detector.

Will Minelab metal detectors find treasure?
I have found more pieces of treasure than I can count using my Minelab machines. Yes they do find treasure, and at times these machines can find treasure very, very deep. I

have recovered targets over 2 feet deep with my Minelab machines on the beach. They are powerful once you learn what they are telling you. Coins, gold, jewelry, silver and relics. I have found them all with my Minelab metal detectors.

Who will benefit the most with A Minelab metal detector?
Anyone who uses a Minelab machine will increase their odds of finding some great treasure. Some of the more advanced machines do have a learning curve, but once you have a good understanding of the machine, they are hard to beat. It all boils down to knowing what that machine is trying to tell you.

You can't go wrong with a Minelab. They have entry level machines that are fun and easy to use, and they have more advanced machines that will recover all sorts of treasure in different ground conditions.

Official company website:
http://www.minelab.com/

Teknetics Metal Detectors

Teknetics metal detectors are manufactured by First Texas Products. This is the same company that manufactures Bounty Hunter and Fisher Labs metal detectors as well.

The Teknetics product line boasts a wide range of features with a simple turn on and go operation. Their simplicity makes them very popular. You will spend far less time trying to learn how to use these machines and more time recovering buried treasure. Their smaller price tag makes it very easy to jump right into the hobby of metal detecting.

Will Teknetics metal detectors find treasure?
Yes they will. Every machine from their entry level machines to their more advanced machines that offer great pinpointing and target separation will increase your odds of finding treasure.

Who will benefit the most with A Teknetics metal detector?
Teknetics machines are great for anyone who wants to get started metal detecting without spending a lot of money. They have some of the lowest priced machines on the market today.

While these lower priced machines will find treasure, you do get what you pay for when it comes to metal detecting. If you are looking for a machine with a small price tag that is easy to use, then this is it. Many Teknetic machines have the same exact features as the Bounty Hunter machines and they are both manufactured by the same company.

Official company website:
http://www.tekneticst2.com/

Tesoro Metal Detectors

Tesoro makes some great metal detectors. What would you expect from a company whose name means treasure in Spanish?

Tesoro has some really interesting history in the metal detecting world. Jack Gifford, the founder of the company worked for Bounty Hunter. He engineered some of their best machines, but he eventually decided to head out on his own and start Tesoro.

He had a simple goal in mind. He wanted to manufacture a metal detector that would use the best technology, provide maximum sensitivity, be strong, rugged, lightweight and easy enough for anyone to use them while keeping an affordable price tag.

Their first metal detector called the Deep Search VI managed to accomplish all of that and more. Tesoro machines still manage to bring all of these qualities to the table today.

There is one thing that is truly unique about Tesoro metal detectors. At the time of this writing, Tesoro was the only metal detector manufacturer to offer a lifetime warranty on their products. This is the reason I purchased my first Tesoro metal detector. I never had to use the warranty and my machine put plenty of treasure in my pockets.

Will Tesoro metal detectors find treasure?
Tesoro means treasure. Of course these machines will find treasure. The entry level machines are great at uncovering buried treasures, and some of the more advanced machines are as well. If you own a Tesoro, you will find plenty of treasure.

Who will benefit the most with a Tesoro metal detector?
Tesoro makes a great line of metal detectors that will help anyone find some great treasure. They are very easy to use. They weigh almost nothing. They are very affordable and they have lifetime warranties. What else could you ask for?

Official company website:
http://tesoro.com/

Whites Metal Detectors

Yet another great contender in the wide world of metal detector manufacturing. Whites has been manufacturing high quality metal detectors since 1950. All of their machines are manufactured in their home town of Sweet Home, Oregon. That's right, they are made in America.

From their entry level models to their more advanced models, Whites pretty much has the metal detecting hobby covered. Most people who use a Whites machine never end up touching anything else. The company's tagline or motto just about sums it up for you. "Serious treasure hunting that's fun for everyone." You can't go wrong with a Whites metal detector.

Will a Whites metal detector find treasure?
Whites offers a metal detector for every type of metal detecting scenario, and they will all find treasure as long as you put some time into hunting. From the rough waves of the ocean to the coin filled tot lots, if you are swinging a Whites metal detector, then you will find some good stuff.

Who will benefit the most with a Whites metal detector?
Whites prides itself on quality, durability and ease of use. Their entry level metal detectors are more than affordable, and they make metal detecting fun. They can be an excellent entry point into the field of metal detecting. They

also have some more advanced models that will help a seasoned pro find even more valuable treasure. They are great for the first timer, or the seasoned pro!

Official company website:
http://www.whiteselectronics.com/

XP Metal Detectors

XP metal detectors have done something that no other metal detecting manufacturer has done as of this writing. They have invented the world's first wireless metal detector. There are no wires at all. The coil and the control box have no wires, and the headphones are wireless as well. This makes the machine quite a bit lighter, and believe it or not wires do get tangled from time to time. They also break. No wires means less trouble, but as of this writing only one model is wireless.

XP metal detectors are manufactured in France, but there are plenty of great distributors all over the globe. The people that have been lucky enough to get their hands on an XP machine swear by it. They are amazed by its ability to locate deep treasure.

Will XP metal detectors find treasure?
To put it simply. Yes they will.

Who will benefit the most with a Whites metal

detector?

I would not recommend an XP machine for a first timer. These machines are geared more towards the people who have been metal detecting for quite a while. If you don't mind learning as you go, then you can't go wrong with a XP metal detector.

Official company website:
http://www.xpmetaldetectors.com/

Metal Detector Types

As if the metal detector manufacturer list did not offer you enough choices, you also need to choose what type of metal detector you want to purchase. When I say "type" I mean function.

There are several very different types of machines out there, and most of them have been designed for a very specific purpose. That is why it is very important to know why and where you plan on using a metal detector. If you are planning on searching an ocean beach for long lost pirate treasure, then you need a machine that has been specifically designed for this purpose. An entry level machine might give you nothing but trouble.

You might be saying to yourself, "Why don't these metal detector manufacturers just make a machine that does it all?" Many of them do, and you will pay a pretty penny for a top of the line machine that has the ability to work in multiple terrain types.

If you just plan on hunting some local parks, you don't need all of those bells and whistles. Here are the different types of metal detectors that are geared towards a very specific type or style of metal detecting.

Metal Detectors Designed for Gold!

This gold nugget is known as the Mojave Nugget. As of this writing, it is the largest gold nugget found in the United States using a metal detector. It weighs a massive 1660 troy ounces. (52kg) Could you imagine unearthing that thing with your metal detector?

Metal Detectors Designed for Gold!

Gold is on the top of every metal detecting enthusiasts list. There is nothing quite as thrilling as seeing some shiny yellow metal being pulled from the earth. I have recovered gold on countless occasions, and I can tell you from experience that it never gets old.

Won't all metal detectors find gold?
That is kind of a trick question because it has a yes and no answer. While all metal detectors will respond to gold, there are some on the market that have been specifically designed to find gold in extreme situations. These are the machines that modern gold prospectors use, and there is a very good reason for this.

Modern gold jewelry is not 100% pure gold. In the United States, most gold is 14k (14 karat). This means that the piece of jewelry is 58% gold. The rest of the jewelry is made of other metals. Pure gold is just too soft to manufacture jewelry. It would bend and break.

In Europe, most gold is 18k (18 karat). 18K jewelry is 75% gold. If you are anything like me, then you might be thinking about jumping on a plane and flying to Europe for some jewelry detecting! 18K is always better than 14k!

The type of gold that you find while gold prospecting is pure gold, and it exists in some really harsh conditions. I am not talking about harsh conditions that make it difficult on the human body, although sweating your life away in the desert is pretty harsh. I am talking about harsh ground conditions.

If you were to take an entry level metal detector out looking for gold nuggets, there is a really good chance you won't find anything but trouble. Gold is almost always found in **heavily mineralized ground conditions**. What exactly does that mean you ask?

There are two types of heavily mineralized ground conditions. Ferrous or ground that is filled with tiny little magnetic iron particles is one type, and If you dragged a magnet through this type of ground, you would find plenty of small iron pieces stuck to the magnet.

The other type of mineralized ground is conductive salts, and to make things even worse, most heavily mineralized ground conditions consist of both! Your average entry level or even multi-purpose metal detector can't see through the tiny little magnetic iron pieces or the conductive salts. You will be digging nothing but false signals everywhere!

A metal detector that has been designed to work in these harsh conditions can see right through all of the conductive salts and tiny iron particles making it much easier to pick out all of that pure gold. There is nothing quite as thrilling as plucking a good sized gold nugget from the earth, and that is exactly what these types of metal detectors have been designed to do.

Beach Hunting Metal Detectors

The beach is one of my favorite places to go metal detecting because you just never really know what you are going to find when you swing your coil over the sand. I have found everything that you can imagine metal detecting the beach, and everything about hunting on the beach is different. You could write an entire book on the subject. Wait a minute. I did write an entire book about metal detecting on the beach. **Shameless self promotion alert.**

Metal Detecting the Beach

You can most likely find **Metal Detecting the Beach** the same exact place you found this book. Amazon carries it in both print and paperback.

Beach Hunting Metal Detectors

Okay the commercial is over, now back to beach hunting metal detectors!

There is no rule that says you can't take your average entry level metal detector to the beach. You will have plenty of fun, and you will find some good stuff, but you could face some problems.

If your beach is a freshwater beach, then just make sure your metal detector can get wet. If it can, then you will be fine. If you are thinking about taking your metal detector to a saltwater beach, then you will need a machine that has been specifically designed for this purpose, but why? Here is the perfect example.

I was metal detecting the beach one afternoon when I noticed a man with an entry level metal detector. He was digging like crazy. He noticed me watching him from a distance and he waved for me to come over. I turned off my metal detector and approached him.

He looked at me and said, "Could you help me find this?" He pointed to a giant hole he had been digging for quite some time. He said, "I keep digging and I keep getting signals all over the place, but I can't seem to find them."

I knew what was going on here, but just to make sure I turned on my machine and went over the giant hole he had been digging. Just as I thought. There was not any metal anywhere where he was digging. I turned off my metal detector and gave him the bad news.

I said, "There is no metal here." The guy just looked at me dumbfounded and said, "But my machine keeps beeping right here!" I hate being the bearer of bad news, but I had to explain what was going on.

His metal detector was not designed for saltwater beaches. His machine was getting false signals from the salt and minerals. When he removed a little bit of sand, he exposed the wet salty sand beneath. He had been digging something that did not even exist for the past two hours.

I told him that his machine would work fine as long as he stayed away from the wet sand. His reply was, "That doesn't leave me very many places to detect on the beach, does it?" I felt bad telling him the truth. It crushed his spirit and he walked away like a dog that has been scolded.

This is what happens when you use a machine that has not been designed for saltwater beaches on a saltwater beach. If you must metal detect on a salt water beach, invest some money in a machine that can handle it.

I have said this time and time again. Your metal detector will quickly pay for itself on the beach as long as you put some time into learning your machine and learning how to hunt on the beach.

My book, Metal Detecting the Beach is a great place to

start if you are interested. I share some great stories of the things I have found, but I also explain why and how I found them. I also tell you how to hunt the beach.

Underwater Metal Detectors

If you are a scuba diver, then you may want to buy a metal detector that you can take deep down under the surface of an ocean, river or lake. These are highly specialized machines that can withstand the pressure that deep water can produce. Taking your average entry level metal detector deep underwater is a bad idea.

While there are quite a few metal detectors out there that are waterproof, there are only a handful of them that can go deeper than 15 feet. (4.5 meters) Pay very close attention to the maximum depth suggestions for your metal detector.

The small selection makes it easier to choose which underwater metal detector is best for you.

Relic Metal Detectors

Relic hunting is extremely exciting. Where else can you unearth a piece of history that has not seen light for hundreds or maybe even thousands of years? That is the reality of relic hunting. One day you could find a tiny fired musket ball that is hundreds of years old, and the next day you could be digging up a cannon ball that was fired from a pirate's ship.

Relic hunting is fun and addictive, and if you want to find the deep targets you will need a machine that has been designed specifically for this purpose.

What makes a relic metal detector different?

A lot of the great relics that are being recovered come from highly mineralized ground. It seems like all the good treasure is hiding in this type of ground doesn't it?

Why not just use a gold or beach metal detector for relic hunting then? Well you can, but most relics are made from iron, steel or brass. Machines that have been designed for gold prospecting discriminate most of these metals out. The same goes for metal detectors that have been designed for beach hunting. Although many of these modern machines have relic hunting modes where nothing is being discriminated.

I found all of the relics in the following picture using a

multi-purpose machine in relic mode.

Relic metal detectors have been designed to use lower frequencies that respond really well to iron, steel and brass. My dad always used to say, "You need the right tool for the job." This is especially true when it comes to metal detecting. If you want to successfully uncover long lost relics, then you will need a machine that has been designed to do so.

Coin Shooting Metal Detectors

If you skipped over the learning the lingo section of this book, then you may not know what coin shooting means. Coin shooting is using a metal detector to locate nothing but older coins. It can be extremely fun uncovering coins that have been hidden in the earth for hundreds of years, and it can be extremely addictive as well. Once you uncover an old piece of silver, you will be hooked. Imagine what it would be like to uncover an old gold coin!

If you spend a good amount of time with just about any metal detector, then you will learn how to locate coins with it. However, there are some machines on the market that seem to work better at finding old coins. These machines could be thought of as coin magnets, and they will quickly pay for themselves.

Good coin hunting machines also have the ability to discriminate metals like iron even when they are located right next to an old coin. This is a huge bonus that makes it so much easier to determine whether or not you should be trying to retrieve a target. The less expensive coin hunting machines may not have the ability to do this. Iron targets may mask a valuable silver coin that is a few inches away.

Coin shooting can be a great entry point into the world of metal detecting, and there are plenty of entry level and multi-purpose machines that will help you uncover coins that are hundreds of years old.

Multi-purpose Metal Detectors

This is just a very small sample of the treasure I have found with my multi-purpose metal detector.

These are the machines that can get it all done. You could think of these machines as the Swiss Army knife of metal detectors because they have the ability to do so many things at once. Most multi-purpose machines will find coins, gold, silver, relics and some of them will even function in highly mineralized soil conditions. There are also a few that are waterproof as well. These are powerful metal detectors that are loaded with functions.

I own one, and it is by far my favorite machine, but there are a few pros and cons to owning a multi-purpose metal detector. Let's look at the possible problems you might be facing with a multi-purpose metal detector.

The first and most obvious downfall is the price. Most multi-purpose metal detectors will cost you quite a bit of money. Notice how I said, "most." Not all of them are expensive, but you get what you pay for. I always recommend getting the best metal detector that you can afford. One good find will pay for the entire thing.

The other not so obvious downfall to owning a metal detector that does everything is the somewhat steep learning curve. Being able to function perfectly in different soil conditions, and target very specific items means there will undoubtedly be a lot of settings to go through.

More knobs, buttons and settings can equal more confusion. This can quickly suck all of the fun out of the hobby. There is nothing worse than digging hole after hole and recovering nothing because you don't understand what your machine it telling you. The frustration is enough for most people to give up all together.

The benefits of a multi-purpose machine far outweigh the potential problems you will face. While most multi-purpose machines can have a challenging learning curve, you don't have to be a computer geek or a rocket scientist to figure them out. All it takes is a little bit of time and patience.

The first thing you will want to do is get that machine out there and start digging up treasure. You will want to justify the cost, and you will be eager to pay for that shiny new metal detector with the treasure you find. Thoughts of gold, silver, old coins and relics will be dancing through your head.

Don't rush it. This is not a race. The time you spend learning your new multi-purpose metal detector is time well spent. Once you master a multi-purpose machine, there is no stopping you from finding the world's greatest treasures.

The other obvious advantage is a metal detector that can do it all. Imagine a metal detector that works on land, in the water, at the beach, at a park, in highly mineralized ground conditions, has a visual identification, an audio identification, a built in GPS and the ability to fine tune every single setting on the machine to your own personal liking.

That is the power that only a multi-purpose metal detector can bring you. These are serious metal detectors for people who don't mind spending a little bit of time learning how they work. Your efforts and patience will be greatly rewarded.

Metal Detectors for Kids

Metal detecting is one of the best hobbies for children. It has so many great benefits for young minds. It gets them outside in the fresh air and sunshine. We all know this is something that kids do less of on a daily basis. Sitting glued to a television, computer, cell phone or a video game is not all that healthy.

Metal detecting gets children out in the real world. They get to explore and be young adventurers. Who knows what they may discover. They also get some much needed exercise as well.

There is another great benefit to kids metal detecting, and that benefit is the value of history. This is very important. Every piece of buried treasure comes with its very own unique story, and you can help tell the story.

Metal detecting makes what would otherwise be a boring old history lesson into an exciting adventure that ends with a piece of physical history that you can hold in your hands.

Keep Them Smiling
Kids love finding buried treasure, but there are two things that will make them lose interest very quickly: A machine that is too difficult to use, and a lack of treasure. Keep things simple, and children will love every minute of it. You may also need to bury some treasure around the yard to keep them entertained.

There are a few metal detectors out there that have been specifically designed for children, but just about any entry level machine will get the job done. Kids just want to be able to turn the machine on and listen for a beep. It is that simple.

The good thing about these entry level machines is the small price tag. You don't have to worry about wasting a lot of money on something that your child may lose interest in.

How Does This Thing Work?

As if the metal detector types and brands were not enough, there are also several very different technologies powering each of these machines. Each major manufacturer will have their own technologies at work deep inside each of their flagship machines. This type of competition amongst metal detector manufacturers makes it great for consumers like us.

Each metal detector manufacturer is trying to outdo each other. The end result of this constant competition are the advanced machines that we use to locate treasure. Lucky us, but what is happening underneath the buttons and knobs? How does this machine do what it does? The answer to this question is frequencies.

When you power on your favorite metal detector, the search coil goes to work. It creates an electromagnetic field that penetrates the surface of the earth. The electromagnetic field consists of different frequencies. Each metal detector manufacturer uses different electronics to transmit these frequencies into the ground.

When these frequencies come into contact with a metal object, something happens. The metal object creates its own electromagnetic field that bounces back towards the metal detector coil. The metal detector coil is designed to pick up these secondary frequencies and process them into

How Does This Thing Work?

information that we can work with. See the image below.

How Does This Thing Work?

That information may be an audible beep, a number or an image on a screen. This information is what we use to determine that a target is buried somewhere under the coil of our metal detector. Your metal detector is not only sending out massive amounts of frequencies. It is also receiving them as well. Check out the image below.

I have often wondered how certain animals respond to these electromagnetic frequencies. I have spent a lot of time metal detecting in and around salt water beaches. I have seen my fair share of sharks while metal detecting these beaches. Sharks are known to respond to electrical impulses in the water around them. This is how they locate their prey.

How does a shark see a metal detector emitting all of these frequencies? If you happen to figure this out and invent the world's first working shark repelling device based on this concept, remember where you got the idea.

Which frequencies work best for treasure hunting?
It would be nice if every metal object reacted to the same frequencies, but that is not the case. That would make things too easy for metal detector manufacturers. Different frequencies have very different effects on the ground and metal objects buried.

Low frequencies are great at going very deep. They respond well to larger objects too. Low frequencies are excellent at locating big items and highly conductive metals like gold, silver and copper. This may sound like the winning choice, but low frequencies are not very good at locating smaller objects.

Medium range frequencies are great for all purpose general metal detecting. They go deep and they respond well to both large and small targets.

High frequencies are great at finding smaller things like small gold nuggets and thin gold chains.

So it looks like you have another choice on your hands. Should you get a machine that uses low, medium or high frequencies? Luckily there are machines on the market that can handle all of them at once! These are the more expensive multi-purpose machines that have been designed to work in multiple ground conditions on multiple targets.

Which Metal Detector Is the Best?

So now that you know about all of the major metal detector manufacturers, the different types and how different frequencies respond to different types of metals, you might be asking yourself this question. Which metal detector is the best? Unfortunately there is no real answer to this question. The best metal detector is the one that works the best for you.

Choose a metal detector that has been designed to do the type of treasure hunting that you will be doing the most. Don't buy a metal detector that has been designed for saltwater use if you live 1000 miles or 1600 kilometers from the nearest ocean, and don't buy a multi-purpose machine if you only plan on hunting for small gold nuggets in the middle of the desert.

If you are not sure you will like the hobby of metal detecting, then don't spend a fortune on a machine that is only going to collect dust in your closet because you got tired of digging up trash. Metal detecting is just like anything else in life. You have to go through some trash before you get to the good stuff below!

Take your time and research your first machine, and when it arrives, get to know it very well. Spend some time outside in the great wide open looking for treasure. Enjoy the hunt. Enjoy being outside. The more time you spend with your metal detector, the better you will get.

You will soon know exactly what your machine is trying to tell you. Your time and patience will be well rewarded. Once you get hooked on digging up treasure, then you can upgrade to some of the fancier machines on the market that have all the bells and whistles.

Buying Your First Metal Detector

You have done all of your research and finally decided on a specific brand and model of metal detector. You are 100% certain that this is the machine for you. Perfect! You are ready to make the purchase, but where do you go to buy this thing?

If you have chosen an inexpensive entry model metal detector, then you may or may not be able to walk into a local department store and make your purchase. You may even know of a local sporting goods store that sells metal detectors. Great! Go for it, but if you have chosen a more expensive model, then there is a really good chance that you won't find it in a local store.

There are a handful of metal detector stores out there that sell nothing but metal detectors and metal detecting supplies, but these stores are few and far between. The chances of there being one of these stores within a reasonable driving distance of your home are slim. This leaves you with only one option. You will have to purchase your new machine either over the phone, or on the Internet.

I happen to live about 30 miles from a metal detecting specialty store, but I have purchased every single one of my metal detectors over the phone, or on the Internet. Why did I do this? I did this to save money. I always found much better deals this way.

Should you buy a used metal detector over the internet?

Being able to purchase a metal detector on the Internet brings up some very interesting points. The most notable being: Should I buy a used metal detector over the Internet.

I bought my second machine on Ebay. It was used and I was 100% satisfied with the purchase. I was able to get an older machine in excellent working condition for half of what I would have paid for a new one. You just have to be smart about who you are buying the metal detector from, and you have to realize what is at stake.

There is a really good chance the used purchase will not come with any type of warranty. Are you okay with that? I was.

Ask as many questions as you possibly can. Ask for pictures of the metal detector. If you and the seller are local, arrange for a meeting where you can see the machine in action. If you are not local, then ask the seller if they would record a video of the machine in action and either post it to youtube.com, or send it directly to you. Research the sellers reputation. Don't be afraid to poke and pry. In the end, your research will be well worth the extra bit of work.

Also be mindful of how you pay for the metal detector.

Buying Your First Metal Detector

When I purchased mine from Ebay, the seller stated that there would be no returns. I paid for the transaction using Paypal. Paypal gives you some protection in this type of situation. If you are not happy with the item, or it is not as described you can dispute the transaction.

In my case, if the metal detector did not work upon arrival, I would have disputed the purchase. Luckily, it was in good shape. That was over six years ago, and the machine is still kicking. I won't tell you how much treasure I have found with this machine either. You will just get jealous!

This is an added layer of protection for buyers. Keep this in mind. Also, remember to research this fact before you take my word for it. Policies change every single day. If you plan on paying for a used metal detector with Paypal, look over their seller protection policy first!

Buying used could also become a huge nightmare for you. If you are not comfortable with the idea, then don't do it. People have had horrible experiences buying used metal detectors on the Internet.

Where else can you find good used metal detectors?
Ebay is not the only place where you can find some really great deals on used metal detectors. You could also try looking at Craigslist.com in your local area. You may be able to find some great deals there. Just be cautious of who you are dealing with.

There are some online metal detector vendors that offer used merchandise as well, and you will find a handful of online metal detecting forums where people buy and sell all sorts of things like treasure and used metal detectors. I will list these forums a little later in the book in the chapter called **Join the Community**.

Buying new?
I have also purchased some machines brand new. I also made these purchases over the phone, or on the Internet and I could not be happier with my purchases. Here is a list of some of the more popular Internet vendors in no particular order. Please note that phone numbers and websites change on a daily basis.

Amazon.com
Yes they do sell just about everything, including metal detectors.

KellyCo
website: http://www.kellycodetectors.com/
phone number: 888-535-5926
Location: 105 Belle Ave
Winter Springs, FL 32708

Big Boy's Hobbies
website: http://www.bigboyshobbies.net/
phone number: 1-405-206-9010
email: bart@bigboyshobbies.net
contact person: Bart Davis

location: Moore, Oklahoma

Fort Bedford Metal Detectors
website: http://www.fortbedfordmetaldetectors.com/
phone number: 814-215-1732
location: 190 Oak Shade Road
Alum Bank, PA 1552

Metal Detecting Stuff
website: http://metaldetectingstuff.com/
phone number: 832-928-9135
location: 22820 Interstate 45 N.
Building 3B
Spring, Texas 77373

Vance Metal Detecting
website: http://www.vancemetaldetecting.com/
phone number: 502-262-0356

Treasure Mountain Metal Detectors
website: http://treasuremtndetectors.com/
phone number: 865-394-5200

Miller MDZ
website: http://www.millermdz.net/
phone number: 610-406-7136
email: tom@millermdz.net

Belda's Gold & Treasure
website: http://www.goldbummin.com/

phone number: 888-301-8552
email: goldbummin@gmail.com

Windy City Detector Sales & Rentals
website: http://windycitydetectors.com/
phone number: 773-774-5445

Detector Depot
website: http://detectordepot.com/
phone number: 865-789-8990
email: info@detectordepot.com
location: 8895 Town & Country Circle Knoxville, TN 37923

North Georgia Relics
website: http://www.northgeorgiarelics.com/
phone: 706-264-6011
email: northgeorgiarelics@gmail.com
location: 7579 Nashville Street
Ringgold, GA 30736

Metal Detecting Accessories

Yes, there are metal detecting accessories. Whether or not you need any of them is completely up to you. I have learned over time that there are quite a few metal detecting accessories that I just can't live without. You could call them the "simple bare necessities." That reminds me of a song.

Just like the initial metal detecting purchase, there are two ways that you can go about getting accessories. You can wait and see which ones you actually need, or you can go out and purchase every one in existence. There is nothing like being properly prepared, but on the other hand, there is such a thing as too much.

Believe it or not, metal detecting can get tiring. You want to lighten the load, or you may not be able to hunt for extended periods of time. It is a good idea to start out with just some of the basics and work your way up as you go. Here are some of the basic metal detecting accessories.

- Sunglasses
- Hat
- Water
- Food or snacks
- Sunblock
- Recovery tools

This is just a basic list of what I call the essentials. There are plenty more accessories out there that you may or may not need. Here are some of the other common metal detecting accessories on the market.

Waterproof Cell Phone Case

I do use one of these for every hunt because I always have my phone with me. The case I use only cost a few dollars, and I can wear it around my neck. This keeps my hands free to recover treasure.

Backpack or Finds Pouch

If you have a lot of accessories, then a backpack is a necessity. It allows you to carry all of your stuff right on your back. You can also use it to store all of the treasures that you find. That brings me to my next point, a finds pouch.

Some hunters will wear a finds pouch that hooks around their waste. I personally have never used one. I just fill my pockets with treasure!

However, there have been times when I have recovered items that were too big to keep in my pocket. That is where the backpack comes in handy.

GPS

If you are doing some hardcore metal detecting way out in the middle of nowhere, you may find a GPS to be very helpful. There are a few metal detectors on the market today that have built in GPS tracking systems. I own one of them. It is a great feature, and it means I don't need a stand alone GPS device to weigh me down.

Metal Detector Bag or Case
A metal detector bag makes it easy to carry all of your stuff, and it gives you a little extra protection in ways you may not have thought of. Leaving an expensive metal detector in the backseat of your car is just asking for trouble. Thieves know a good opportunity when they see it. Putting your metal detector in a bag makes it easy to carry, and it hides it from the eyes of those nasty thieves!

Support Strap
There are some metal detectors out there that weigh more than others. The heavier machines can be difficult to use for extended periods of time. That is why they make support straps or support systems. These unique straps help support some of the extra weight. This makes it so much easier to swing your metal detector for hours.

Batteries
The more expensive metal detectors on the market come with rechargeable battery packs, but it never hurts to have a spare battery pack. You never know when yours may stop working.

The same goes for metal detectors that run on regular store bought batteries. Always make sure you have a backup set of batteries in your backpack, metal detecting bag or finds pouch.

Books

You have the only metal detecting book that you will ever need, and you are reading it right now. I am just kidding with you. If you like to read, then buy as many metal detecting books as possible. Knowledge is power. Arm yourself with plenty of metal detecting books and study them all.

Coils and Coil Covers

Some metal detectors allow you to switch coils. If this is the case, then bringing an assortment of different sized coils may be helpful. The same could be said of coil covers. A coil cover will prevent you from scratching your coil up. Most high end machines come with a coil cover.

Compass

You never know when you may get lost in the woods. A compass should be part of any basic survival kit.

Magnifying Glass or Jeweler's Loupe

This is a must have accessory, especially if your eyes are not what they used to be. (That would be me!) I carry a small jeweler's loupe with me everywhere. They only cost a couple of dollars, and they make it so easy to read stamps or markings on jewelry. They also make it easy to see dates and fine details on finds. You can find them on Amazon, Ebay and other websites for just a few dollars.

Gloves

Gloves are very important. Not only will they keep your hands warm and clean, but they will also protect your hands from sharp objects that may be buried with your treasure.

Knee Pads

You will quickly notice that you will be spending a lot of time on your knees looking in holes. Knee pads will keep your knees comfortable and they will keep your pants from getting stained.

If you have ever had the misfortune of kneeling on a small rock right on the edge of your knee cap, then you will know why knee pads are necessary. Has this happened to me? Why do you think I am suggesting you get some knee pads?

Towel or Old Shirt

There will be times when your target is buried deep in a well manicured lawn. Placing a towel on the ground next to the hole will give you a place to put all the dirt you have to remove. I will go into detail with images in the chapter on recovery.

Diamond Tester

Why would you need a diamond tester when you are metal detecting? You will eventually find some diamond jewelry. A diamond tester will tell you if the stones in your treasure are authentic diamonds.

Display Case
Where else are you going to store and showcase all of your great treasures?

Flashlight
If you plan on doing any hunting at night, then a flashlight is a must have.

Gold Test Kit
There will be times when you find some gold jewelry. It may or may not be marked.

Either way, a gold test kit will help you determine if the item is really made from gold. Most test kits come with several variants that allow you to determine the purity of your gold. For example: 10k, 14k, 18k, or pure. Be careful using these kits because they use acid in different strengths to determine what type of gold you have.

Gram Scale
A good digital gram scale will tell you exactly how much gold, silver or platinum you have.

Rain Jacket
You never know when it is going to rain.

Camera
I always like to bring a good camera with me. I will often take pictures and even record video right there on the spot

when I find a piece of treasure. My cell phone doubles as a camera and a video camera. I always carry a GoPro waterproof high definition camera with me too.

Protection

I am sure you already know this, but it is a dangerous world out there. Bring some type of protection with you while hunting, especially if you are hunting alone.

That about covers all of the accessories that you may or may not need. As you spend more time using your metal detector, it will become obvious which accessories will become the most important to you.

Recovery Tools

Your fancy new metal detector will tell you where the treasure is, but it won't dig it up for you. It is up to you to retrieve that long lost piece of treasure, and in order to do that you are going to need some recovery tools.

This chapter does not cover the art of recovery itself, and believe me there is an art to carefully recovering your treasure. This chapter is simply to inform you of the different types of recovery tools.

Next to your metal detector, your recovery tools will become your most important tools. Get the best recovery tools that you can afford. Your body will thank you later.

Shovel
A basic shovel will help you unearth all types of treasures. Your basic shovel will work fine, but there are some better options out there. You may even decide to make your own specialty shovel after looking over these options.

Specialty Shovels
There are several types of shovels that have been specifically designed for metal detecting. Choosing the right specialty tool for the job will depend on where you plan on metal detecting.

For instance, if you plan on hunting the beach, then a beach scoop is a must. If you plan on searching for relics deep in the woods, then a relic hunting shovel is the right tool for the job.

There are a few brands worth looking at, and almost all of the metal detecting vendors that I listed above will carry them. Lesche makes some great recovery tools, and Sampson does too.

Hand Digger
This is a small hand held shovel that has been designed specifically for metal detecting. Most hand held diggers look kind of like a knife. Some of them feature a serrated edge for easy digging and plug cutting. Here is a picture of my trusty Lesche hand digger.

Probes
Using a probe takes some serious skill. A probe is similar to a screwdriver, and it allows a person to remove a coin from the soil without digging a hole. I will cover this more in the chapter about recovery methods.

Pinpointer
A pinpointer makes finding your buried piece of treasure so much easier. It is essentially a small hand held metal detector. You may not see the need for one of these right away, but they sure do come in handy when you start trying to locate deep items.

Hoes & Picks

If you happen to be hunting in an area where the soil is tough and full of rocks, then a pickaxe is a must. It will make recovery so much easier.

Small Hand Held Folding Landscaping Saw

This one is something that a lot of hunters don't carry with them. I didn't until an old friend of mine told me just how valuable these little saws can be.

There is a good chance that you will encounter plenty of roots that will prevent you from recovering your piece of treasure. A small hand held saw like the Silky **Folding Landscaping Hand Saw** will make quick work of these pesky roots that always seem to get in the way.

Strong Magnet

A strong magnet can be an invaluable tool for helping you retrieve items that may be just beyond your reach. Attach the magnet to your pick ax, and you can easily use it to reach places where your arms can't quite go. The magnet is also a great way to determine if an item is iron or not. You may even be able to use the magnet to pull the buried item out of the ground. A good, strong rare earth magnet can do this without any problems at all.

Having the right recovery tools not only makes it easy to retrieve deep buried targets, but they also help you retrieve the target without doing any damage to it or the surrounding area.

Recovery Tools

As you spend more time metal detecting, you will slowly start to increase your metal detecting recovery tool arsenal.

The Rules of the Road

There is no "written" set of rules that you must adhere to, but there are a few things that you should keep in mind at all times when you are metal detecting. These are not rules. They are more like a simple code of ethics.

There are people in government at city, county, state and federal levels who are trying to ban the great hobby of metal detecting. These people have been successful at banning the use of metal detectors in several key places. Let's not give them any fuel for the fire they are building. Following these simple basic rules will help preserve this great hobby for years to come.

Where is metal detecting against the law?
As I have already stated, there are several places where using your metal detector could land you behind bars. You could also lose your metal detecting equipment and your vehicle. Always make sure it is not against the law before you start metal detecting.

Times change, and government officials change the rules all the time. At the time of this writing, the following places are considered off limits to metal detecting. This pertains to the United States only.

- **Some state parks are off limits.** These seem to vary from state to state, and from park to park within each state. It is always best to locate the head ranger at the state park and ask them. You may be required to obtain a permit, or the park may be wide open to metal detecting. Ask first!

- **National Parks are off limits.** At least every single one I have ever been to is, and I have been to quite a few all over the country.
- **Archeological Sites or Sites of Historical Significance** are also off limits.

Know the Local Laws

It is up to you to know your local laws as they pertain to metal detecting and abide by them. Failing to follow the laws will not only get you in some serious trouble, but it will also make it much easier for "the man" to outlaw metal detecting everywhere.

Obtain Permission Before Metal Detecting Private Property

This one is pretty simple. Do not under any circumstances think that it is "okay" to hunt an area of land if you are not the rightful owner. If you are not sure if the land is public or private, then you are better off not hunting the land in question. Get permission from the rightful land owner. If you can manage, get permission in writing.

Do Not Destroy Property!

his may seem like common sense, but don't destroy anything trying to recover a piece of treasure unless you have explicit permission. This includes: trees, shrubs, plants, animals, your neighbor, buildings and lawns.

Fill In All Holes!

The area where you have hunted should not look like a war zone when you are done. The area should look untouched. Fill in all of your holes. This is the most common mistake that people who are new to the hobby make, and it is by far the most common complaint people in government make. For the third time, fill in all your holes.

Avoid Digging Huge Holes!

There are times when digging a huge hole is necessary. You may need to recover a large relic of some sort, but most of the times you don't need to dig a huge hole. Learn to dig the smallest hole possible, and make sure you use the right recovery tool for the job.

Learn how to cut good plugs. Don't worry. I will show you how in a later chapter. Once you get the hang of cutting a good plug, no one will be able to tell that you where ever there.

Remove All Trash!

You are going to find plenty of trash. It is just part of the hobby. Don't put trashy items back in the hole and cover it up. Take the trashy item with you, or drop it in the nearest garbage can.

Be Respectful of Other Metal Detectorists

If you happen to see another person out metal detecting,

keep your distance while your machine is on. Sometimes your machine will cause all sorts of interference with theirs, and don't even think about moving into their spot while they are hunting. If you must approach them, turn your machine off first. When your conversation is over, respect their spot unless they invite you to join the hunt.

Leave Gates and Accesses as You Found Them

This one is pretty simple too. If you are metal detecting an area where you pass through an open gate, leave it open. If you have to pass through a closed gate, make sure you close it when you pass through it.

Report Significant Finds

You may be lucky enough to find some treasure that has massive historical significance. It is up to you to report these types of finds to the proper authorities. Not doing so could earn you a tour with the chain gang if you know what I mean.

As you can see, the metal detecting code of ethics is pretty much common sense. You may also notice that everything listed in the code of ethics has one thing in common: respect. Respect goes a very long way, especially when you are talking about metal detecting.

Where Should You Metal Detect?

Great Finds Are Everywhere!

There is a good chance that you have heard the popular expression, "Don't judge a book by its cover." This expression rings true, and it is great advice when it comes to metal detecting. You can't really look at an area and instantly determine that it will be a bad place to hunt. You have no way of knowing what may or may not have happened at a particular location in the past. Here is the perfect example.

My son and I were metal detecting a section of woods that sees regular use. There is a nature trail and a lot of locals use the trail for things like bike riding, walking and jogging. At first glance, the area seems like a great place for a nature walk and that's about it. You would never think there would be anything of value buried here by just glancing around, but you would be wrong.

We followed the nature trail for quite a while. We were not finding much at all. I decided to venture off the trail and into the woods. Within five minutes I found an area of woods that was simply loaded with good signals. In fact the signals were everywhere. I couldn't move my coil more than 6 inches (15 centimeters) without getting a signal.

The first target we recovered was a bullet. The next target was a bullet casing. The area was loaded with bullets. We couldn't tell the age of the bullets, but our next target gave us a very good clue. It was a coin from the early 1900s. This coin sat buried in this section of woods for around 100 years. I was amazed at our discovery.

The old coin got our blood pumping, and soon my son and I were pulling old coin after old coin out of the ground. Then the targets just stopped. We back tracked through the woods and moved in another direction. The finds continued for a good hour and a half in the other direction, but they were not just coins, there were also plenty of great relics that started to give us a clearer picture of the history in this small area of seemingly empty woods.

The first clue came when we uncovered a large sheet of

metal roofing. Ahhhh! There was a house here at some point in time. Then we started finding old silver spoons. Three of them to be exact. We also uncovered an antique vintage copper flashlight from the early 1930s.

At one point in time, there was a group of people living here in a house, but you would never know it by looking around. The house was gone. Everything that remained was buried beyond sight. The surrounding plants and foliage had taken over any prior signs of civilization. The moral of this story is this. Don't let your eyes tell you an area is no good. Get out there and see what your metal detector tells you. You just might be surprised by what you find.

Start In Your Own Backyard!
There is no better place to get started than right in your own backyard. It doesn't matter how long you have lived at your house. Your backyard could be a literal gold mine, but you will never know unless you get out there and start searching. I have found plenty of great treasure right in my own yard. I even found an old gold ring!

Your backyard is also a great place to get a feel for your metal detector. Go ahead, spend some time in your own yard before you go out for a big hunt. Just be careful of things like: electrical lines, gas lines, phone lines, water lines and sprinkler systems. Cutting into any of these with your recovery tools will cause all sorts of trouble.

Where Should You Metal Detect?

Go Where People Gather
I am sure you can think of plenty of great places where people may gather on a regular basis. Any place where people have spent any considerable amount of time will always be a good spot to metal detect. Here are a few spots that are always worth hunting:

- parks
- sports fields
- schools
- playgrounds or tot lots
- beaches
- rivers
- lakes
- creeks
- campgrounds
- pastures
- fields
- freshly plowed fields
- ghost towns
- battlefields
- fairgrounds
- picnic areas
- swimming holes
- old homes and buildings
- churches
- RV parks
- around old mailboxes
- parking meters

Where Should You Metal Detect?

- hunting or fishing camps
- the woods
- old factories
- mines

While most of these locations may seem rather obvious, there are other locations that offer great metal detecting opportunities that might not be so obvious. Can you guess what the next chapter is about?

Not So Obvious Metal Detecting Location Opportunities

I always try to make it a point to bring my metal detector with me no matter where I go. You just never know when a good metal detecting opportunity may pop up. You may drive by a place and notice an old foundation, or you may happen upon one of the best kept metal detecting secrets that exists: demolition.

I can't tell you how many times I have stopped at areas where an old building has been demolished only to find more than my share of old coins and relics. Of course I made sure it was okay to hunt the area where the building had once been. There are a few other great places just like this one.

Anytime they tear out an old street to pave the new one, you can bet good money that there will be loads of treasure underneath that old street. Just think of how long that road has been there. It may have been there for 20, 40, 50 or 100 years. All of that soil that is freshly exposed from the road tear out has not seen the light of day for a very long time, and you can bet there will be plenty of treasure underneath it.

The same goes for sidewalks that are being removed. If you have your metal detector in your car, then you can stop anytime you see these great opportunities and score plenty of great treasures. You never know when these types of opportunities will show up. Keep your metal detector handy.

Old Trees

Large old trees almost always hold some great treasure tangled somewhere in their massive maze of roots. It can be hard to determine the history of an old tree, but think of the things that may have happened around a tree that is hundreds of years old.

Not So Obvious Metal Detecting Location Opportunities

Think of all the people who may have sat under that tree in order to get some much needed shade. They could have been soldiers, politicians, royalty, Indians or someone with a pocket full of change. I never pass up an opportunity to metal detect around large old trees.

This should give you plenty of great ideas to start hunting. Just remember to always get permission before you start.

Obtaining Permission on Private Property

Most people miss some of the greatest metal detecting opportunities because they simply don't know how to ask for permission, or they fear rejection. The worst thing that can happen is someone can say no. If that's the case, then move on. Don't be afraid to ask someone to hunt their property with your metal detector.

There is a right way and a wrong way to go about this. Here is the wrong way to go about this. Show up at the property wearing old and dirty clothes and say, "Hey can I dig a bunch of holes in your yard looking for gold?" If you do this, you can forget about getting permission. It is all in the presentation.

Look clean, and professional when you approach the person. First impressions are very important here. If you are knocking on a stranger's door, then introduce yourself. Be honest, and tell the property owner that you would be interested in metal detecting their property.

Tell them you won't destroy anything, and in most cases, they will never even know you were there. This is usually all it takes to get permission. It has worked for me about 70% of the time.

One day I decided to bring my son with me because I had located a really good spot to metal detect. It was on private property, and I had to gain permission first. My son was about 8 at the time. We both approached the door, and I introduced myself and my son to the property owner.

I told him that his property had some pretty interesting history. I brought a few older articles with me that explained some of the past history. I told the property owner that my son and I would be interested in metal detecting their property. The property owner smiled and said, "Sure!"

We found quite a few civil war relics that day. I brought quite a few of them back to the property owner who was very happy to have them. I learned two things that day. One: bringing my son seemed to help break the ice. It made the situation less intimidating for everyone, especially the property owner. The second thing I learned was this. Property owners are always very happy to have relics or anything found on their property handed to them.

Getting Your Hands Dirty
There may be a situation or two where you might have to trade or do a little bit of bartering to obtain permission. You may even have to do a little bit of work around the property in order to obtain permission. Don't be afraid to offer to help lend a hand. You will be surprised by how many doors this can open.

Business Cards or Flyers
If you look professional, but down to earth, then obtaining

permission is easy. You could go so far as to have business cards printed that have your name and phone number on them. This can have some drawbacks because the property owner may think you are trying to sell them something.

I have found that bringing a small color flyer with me helps big time. I fill the flyer up with pictures of some of my best finds. The flyer can be an easy way to break the ice. You can direct the property owner's attention to the great items on the flyer while you tell them about every piece of treasure.

You can even go so far as to bring a log book or a finds journal with you. This can really help get the conversation going. The property owner may even have a story or two to tell you about some possible great places to start hunting on their property.

Give a Short Demonstration
Some property owners are so fascinated by the idea of locating treasure on their property that they may even ask for a demonstration. Go for it! Show the property owner exactly how your machine works. You may even want to take them on the hunt with you.

Write a Letter
If you don't like the idea of approaching a stranger's door, then you can break the ice with a well written letter. The letter should have a brief introduction, and then it should quickly get to the point. If you have any interesting

information about the property, you may want to include it in the letter.

With a little bit of practice, you should have no problems obtaining permission to hunt anywhere.

Research

Research is something that a lot of folks don't enjoy, but researching metal detecting locations is a little different. Your research will equal a great payoff. Just think of the history you can uncover if you put some time into researching an area. You may make the greatest metal detecting find of your life, but how do you go about researching?

Start Your Research At Your Local Library
The library can be the best place to start doing some research. You will be pleasantly surprised at the amount of great information that can be found at your local library. Most libraries have plenty of rich history that goes back

hundreds of years.

Start by looking through local history books, and then move to old newspaper articles. Keep your eyes open for things like: areas where there may have been battles, public events and celebrations.

Old maps, atlases and Farmer's Almanacs are also an excellent source of information. Old maps will tell you where things used to be. You may be able to locate old hotels, buildings, parks, stores, restaurants, schools, post offices or an entire city itself. Most cities have been moved at one time or another. If you can locate where a city started, you can bet you will find plenty of great treasure just waiting for you right below the surface.

Local Museums or Historical Societies
Local museums are also an excellent place to start your research. You will find that most local museums have a complete treasure trove of old books that are packed full of juicy metal detecting tidbits. Be ready to take notes when you go, and be ready to find some great spots to metal detect.

The same could be said of any local historical society. They will have a huge amount of information for you to look through. They may even have some older maps that could shed some light on some very promising areas for metal detecting.

Research

You may or may not want to mention metal detecting when you are dealing with the historical society. Some people don't like the idea of someone using a metal detector to uncover treasure.

Listen Up!

Every city has an older crowd. It doesn't matter how big or small the city is. There will always be a few old timers who know where things used to be, these people are always more than eager to share their knowledge with you. All you have to do is pull up a chair and listen.

I have the perfect example. I was metal detecting an area close to a popular beach when an older gentleman approached me. He looked at me and said, "You are in the wrong spot buddy. You need to move two blocks to the east. In the early 1900s there was a casino located right over there." I never knew there was a casino anywhere in the area. I thanked the old timer, and quickly made my way towards the area he pointed out.

I couldn't believe my first target when I pulled it out of the dirt.
It was this 1921 Peace Dollar!

I found plenty more older silver coins in the same area. I still go back to this spot from time to time and manage to pull out a few older coins. All I had to do was listen to what someone was eager to tell me.

Civil War Research

If your type of treasure consists of a bunch of civil war relics and artifacts, then you will need to locate some places that are rich in Civil War history. This is not that hard to do. There are plenty of states where huge battles were fought. Most of these battles are pretty well documented too, but there is one source that has everything that you could ever want to know about the Civil War.

That source is called: The War of the Rebellion. It is a massive compilation of the official records of both the Union and the Confederate armies. There is so much information packed into these books that you could spend a lifetime reading it all. It even has detailed maps that highlight areas of interest. You can search Google for "The War of the Rebellion", or you can use this website: http://ehistory.osu.edu/osu/sources/records/

Either way, this is hands down the best information you will find on the Civil War.

Put Technology to Work
Today it is much easier to research some great places to metal detect using nothing but a computer or a smartphone. The Internet has made anything possible, and it has opened an entire new way to research some potentially great areas to swing your coil.

I have spent countless hours researching new places on the Internet, and it has always paid off very well. One of the easiest ways to start looking for some great places is by using Google Maps or Google Earth. Both of these great tools can give you a bird's eye view of the area around you. You will be amazed at what you can find doing this.

Research

There are avid treasure hunters who have found sunken ships and sunken airplanes off the coast using these tools. People have also been able to find old home sites using these tools as well.

I have located several great places to metal detect just using this technology to look around my home. Once you start looking at the area around you using this awesome satellite technology, an entire new world opens up.

Here is another good example. Recently I was using Google Maps to try and locate some interesting areas to metal detect with my son. I went to maps.google.com and typed in my address. I then changed the view to satellite view.

This gave me an excellent view of the area around my house. I started moving the map around looking for anything that looked interesting. I noticed what looked like a small path off of a local road. I zoomed in. It was a foot path that I had never seen before. I zoomed back out to get a better look.

The foot path went for a few miles through some woods. I could barely see it through the tree tops. The path then went far out into a huge marshland where it seemed to stop.

This looked like the perfect place to try a new hunt. I told my son, and we eagerly drove down the road looking for the foot path. There it was. I parked my truck. We unloaded our gear and started down the foot path.

It didn't take us very long to start finding modern targets. The further down the foot path we went, the older the targets became. It was obvious to me that we were in a very good spot when we started finding old silver coins, and all I did was use Google Maps to locate this area.

There are other great opportunities out there in cyberspace. You just have to get busy looking for them. Just think of it as part of the hunt. Here are some great places for you to start researching on the Internet.

maps.google.com
This is the easiest way to get a bird's eye view of your area.

earth.google.com
This is like Google Maps, but 100 times better. With Google Earth, you can add, edit and do all sorts of great things to a map.

archive.org
This is one of my best kept secrets. There are very few people who use this great free resource. It is a free library that is loaded with old out of print books and maps. You won't believe the amount of great information that is available at archive.org.

Research

You could use these search terms:

civil war maps
old maps
antique maps

You could also start searching using your city or state and the word maps. For instance: If you lived in Chicago, you can search for Chicago maps. The amount of information at this site is truly unbelievable, and it is all there waiting for you to claim it.

BLM Research
The United States Bureau of Land Management is also a great place to start doing some research. They have a huge database of information on old and new mining claims. I have spent countless hours looking through this information. I find it fascinating. At the time of this writing, you could access this information at the following website:
http://www.blm.gov/lr2000/index.htm

Youtube.com
This is yet another great place to start doing some research. Not only can you find tons of great information on history, but you can also find plenty of great videos that can help you learn how to locate even more treasure!

Ghost Towns
These are by far my favorite. You can learn so much from

an old ghost town, and you can find loads of great treasure too. I use this website all the time:
http://www.ghosttowns.com/

It is loaded with great information on old ghost towns that not everyone knows about. You can locate ghost towns by state or province. In some cases, the information you locate here can lead you to plenty of other great sites as well.

Treasure Hunting Magazines
There are several great publications out there that are devoted to helping you find more treasure. You can purchase these magazines individually, or you can order a subscription. These magazines are packed full with great treasure hunting information. Here are some of the top ones worth looking at.

http://www.wetreasures.com/

http://www.americandigger.com/

http://www.losttreasure.com/

http://www.treasurehunting.co.uk/

You can never do too much research. Take your time, and you will be well rewarded

Let's Go Metal Detecting

In case you are wondering, yes that is me in the picture up there, and yes I am that goofy in real life.

The moment has finally arrived. You put some fresh batteries in your brand new metal detector, or you charged up your battery packs. You are now more than eager to get out there and start recovering some long lost treasures.

Before you rush out to that great spot you spent a lot of time researching, there are still a few very important things that you need to take into consideration. You could think of these as tips that will make your first trip metal detecting even more enjoyable.

Slow and Steady Wins the Treasure

Metal detecting is not a race. The faster person does not get the most treasure. In fact, metal detecting is quite the opposite. You need to slow down and make sure your coil covers every single inch or centimeter of ground. Swinging your coil fast will and can cause all sorts of false signals.

Pay close attention to your swing pattern as it relates to your walking speed. I like to try and pretend that I am painting the ground with my metal detector. Try to keep a mental picture in your head of where you swing your coil. Does your walking speed cause you to miss any small areas? For most people just starting out, it does. Any areas you miss with your coil may have some buried treasures. Keep it nice and slow.

Pretty soon you may even find that you have worked into a specific rhythm. Your feet move perfectly with your swing speed, and you never miss even a centimeter of treasure producing ground. I will say it again. Metal detecting is not a race. Keep it nice and slow and you will be well rewarded.

Pay Attention to Your Coil

There are a few other very common problems that I see quite often. The people who are doing these things are the people who wind up finding very little treasure. These common problems specifically address the coil.

First and foremost: keep your coil as close to the ground as possible. You don't know how many times I have seen people swinging their coil 6 inches (15 centimeters) or a foot (30 centimeters) off the ground. This is not beneficial. I repeat, this is not going to help you find anything! Keep your coil as close to the surface of the ground as possible, but **DO NOT SCRAPE YOUR COIL ACROSS THE GROUND!** Not only will you cause damage to your coil, but you will be getting all sorts of false signals too.

The same goes for bumping your coil on rocks, pebbles, roots, bushes and the occasional lawn gnome. All of these instances will cause most metal detectors to produce a false signal.

Your Coil Is Not a Pendulum!

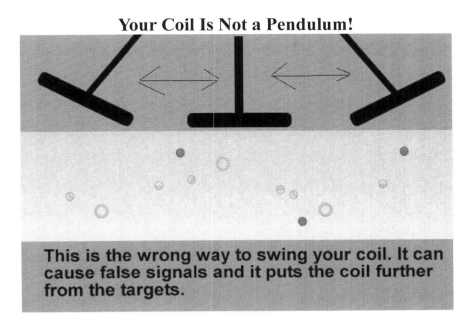

This is the wrong way to swing your coil. It can cause false signals and it puts the coil further from the targets.

Do not swing your coil wildly like a clock pendulum. I see people doing this all the time, and they are making it nearly impossible to locate treasure when their swing reaches the furthest to the right or the left. Keep your coil as close to the ground as possible even when you have reached the furthest point of your swing.

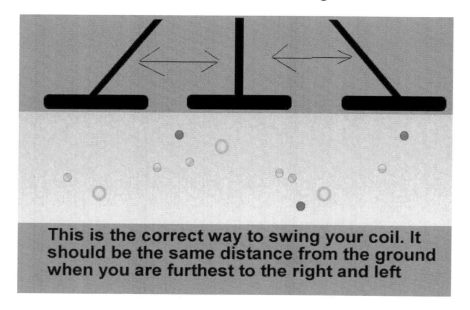

This is the correct way to swing your coil. It should be the same distance from the ground when you are furthest to the right and left

Work Efficiently

There is nothing wrong with grabbing your metal detector and just going for a stroll through a local field or a playground. I enjoy doing this all the time, but there is a way that works much better, especially if the area you are covering is large and open. You need to slowly grid the area. I already mentioned this in the learning the lingo section of the book.

Gridding is really easy and it will ensure that you cover every inch or centimeter of ground. Start on one end of the area and walk in one direction. When you get to the end of the area, move a short distance over and turn around and go back the opposite direction. Your path should form a tight grid over the area.

Once you have finished your grid in one direction, turn and go the opposite way. It can be difficult to understand this concept with just plain old text, so I drew up this handy diagram that makes it easier to understand. This is a bird's eye view of the area. The line is the pattern you will be following.

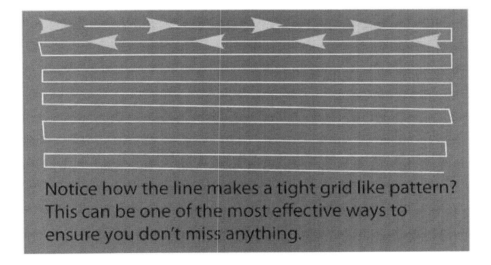

Notice how the line makes a tight grid like pattern? This can be one of the most effective ways to ensure you don't miss anything.

Repeat the pattern in the opposite direction!

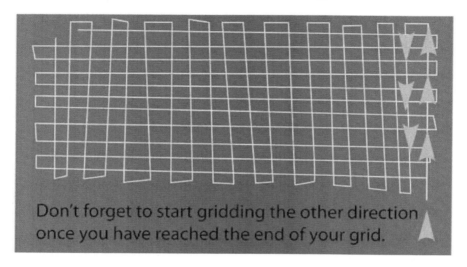

Don't forget to start gridding the other direction once you have reached the end of your grid.

This is by far the most effective way to completely cover an area without missing any possible targets.

Spiraling Outwards

Another method for covering a lot of ground is the spiral. This method is completely different, and it works well if you suspect targets are grouped together. Start hunting the area in any particular pattern until you find a good target. Once you recover the target, keep hunting in a outwards spiral pattern like in the image below.

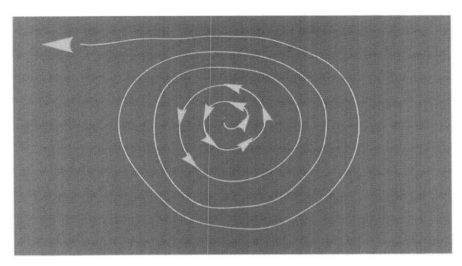

Saving the Best Spots for Last

Saving the best spots for last may sound like a really good idea, but it is not. I had the bright idea to try this one time. I was hunting in an old ball field. There used to be a concession stand in one area of the park. I knew exactly where it was, but I decided to save it for last.

I arrived at the ball field, and I had the entire place to myself. I spent a couple of hours working the ball field. I found a few things, but nothing worth mentioning. I was ready to move over to where the old concession stand used to be. I knew there would be some older coins there because the concession stand was active in the early 1900s.

I was looking forward to going over the area, but when I got over there, someone else was happily digging up all the old coins. Apparently, while I was working over the ball field, someone else showed up and cleaned out the old concession stand area. I learned a very valuable lesson that day. Always go over the good spots first. This includes any places where people may have gathered two days ago, or 200 years ago.

Metal Detecting A Stream, River or Creek

Metal detecting in streams, rivers and creeks can be very productive because not very many people hunt them. You need a waterproof metal detector, and most people prefer to stay dry. Not me. I will go where the treasure is, and I have been greatly rewarded hunting streams, rivers and creeks.

There are a few things to keep in mind when you are doing this. Always put safety first. No amount of treasure is worth losing your life. Be mindful of strong currents, deep holes, flash floods and submerged objects. One slip and fall is all it takes to send you quickly downstream without a paddle.

One of the great things about hunting these types of waterways is the vast amount of targets to be found. Streams, rivers and creeks are full of lost treasures. People have always been attracted to water, and people always tend to lose things in or around these types of waterways.

While you can easily find plenty of targets in the water, there are some things that will greatly improve your finds. You need to be able to read a body of water and understand all of the flows and eddies. It also helps to understand how heavy objects are affected by moving water.

Objects in water only weigh as much as the water they displace. If you have ever tried to lift a very heavy object underwater, then you know exactly what I am talking about. Suddenly that heavy object is not so heavy anymore. This is true with heavy metal objects too.

Fast moving water can easily pick up a heavy object and move it miles downstream, but what do you think happens when the current slows down a bit? Heavier objects tend to settle towards the bottom when this happens. So you need to locate areas where water flow may be slowed by nature.

Depth, bends, submerged objects and eddies can all slow down the flow of a stream, river or a creek. These are the places where all of the heavy metal objects will settle and sink to the bottom.

I have found areas in creeks that have taken days to clean out. It all comes down to learning how to spot these natural areas of slower moving water. Look for sudden changes in depth, submerged objects that change the speed of the water flow and sharp bends and turns. You should be able to see an accumulation of rocks and gravel in these areas. This is a good sign that you are in the right place!

The diagram below is a good example. The arrows represent the direction the water is flowing. The darker spots represent the areas of water where the current slows and heavy objects are deposited. These are great spots to start hunting.

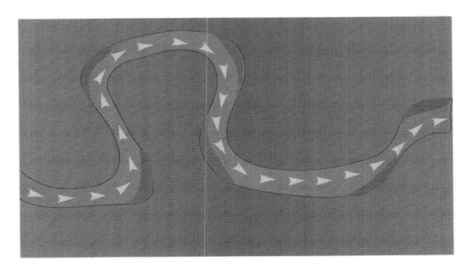

Here is a good example of a stream that is hiding a good spot. Take a look at the picture. The water is flowing in the direction of the arrow. What do you see?

It looks like an ordinary creek doesn't it? Take a look at the next picture where I have highlighted some basic clues.

Why would there be small bubbles and foam on the opposite side of the faster moving water? The next image will show you the answer.

The small bubbles and foam are being caused by an eddy. The water in this part of the creek actually moves in two directions because there is a deep hole on the other side. The additional arrows are highlighting the direction of the water. How do I know this?

When I was standing at the edge of this creek studying the water flow, I was eating an orange. I threw a few pieces of my orange peel in the water upstream and watched them as they moved downstream. Both pieces got caught in an eddy. I will circle the orange peels in the next picture, and I will highlight the deeper spot.

If there were any heavy items moving downstream, they would settle and sink to the bottom in this area. This is the first place I would start hunting. This is exactly how gold prospectors read streams. Now that I think about it. I need to get my gold pan out and head over to this creek.

Learning to spot eddies in the water is another excellent way to locate some great spots. eddies are areas of water where the natural flow of water is changed dramatically. Sometimes the water may even flow in the opposite direction. Eddies appear on the surface of the water as small to medium sized whirlpools. These are good indications of where you should start hunting.

Here is another good example. Take a look at this section of stream.

Go ahead. Study the picture for a little while. Can you spot the very obvious sign?

Metal Detecting A Stream, River or Creek

The circled area of rocks is a very obvious sign. Notice how the rocks extend out into the water a little bit? This entire circled area of the creek is underwater when water levels are high. Excessive rain or a spring thaw would cause this. This area is also right around an inside bend in the creek.

All of those stones fell out of suspension when the water levels dropped. Heavy metals will be deposited right along with them. This is a great place to metal detect, and an even better place to start panning for gold.

Reading an area of water can be difficult at times, but there is a very easy way to spot areas where the water slows and changes directions. Take a handful of leaves and toss them in the water. Pay close attention to how they move downstream. You will quickly see where and how the water moves downstream. You will also be able to quickly see where all the eddies and back flow areas are.

Keep the following tip in mind when hunting streams, rivers, creeks or any body of water.

Any stream, river or creek that is near a well traveled road will be loaded with trash. For some reason people just love to throw their garbage in the water. I am not saying you should not hunt flowing water that is close to busy roads because you should. Just be prepared to dig up a lot of trash in the process. Enough of the water hunting advice. Let's move back to dry land.

The Art of Pinpointing

The Art of Pinpointing

You are ready to start digging up treasure. You have your new metal detector, and you have just located your first target. Congratulations, but how in the world are you supposed to know exactly where it is?

The coil on your metal detector could be anywhere from 4 inches (10 centimeters) to 20 inches (50 centimeters) wide. Your target is somewhere underneath the coil. It is time to pinpoint your target!

The concept behind pinpointing is pretty simple to understand. Pinpointing is using your metal detector to precisely locate your target in the smallest possible area. A small coil makes it easier to pinpoint. Pinpointing with a larger coil can be some what challenging.

Luckily there are quite a few newer machines on the market that have a pinpoint mode. Switching your metal detector to pinpoint mode will make it easier to precisely locate your target. Since every machine is a little different, you will have to refer to your machine's instruction manual in order to learn how to use its pinpoint mode.

Pinpointing is most definitely an art form. It takes some time to learn how to master this important metal detecting technique, but it is a necessity for a few reasons.

The Art of Pinpointing

Being able to accurately pinpoint the location of your target will make recovery faster and easier. It will also mean that you will only have to remove a very small amount of earth to retrieve your target. This makes it really easy to put everything back the way it was and leave no signs that you were ever even there.

People who have mastered pinpointing may not even need to dig a hole in order to retrieve their target. I will talk a little more about that in the chapter on recovery.

Pinpointing Methods
There is more than one way to skin a cat, and there is more than one way to pinpoint a target with your metal detector. Again, I highly recommend that you consult your instruction manual to learn which way the manufacturer suggests you pinpoint using your machine.

Audio Pinpointing
Most modern machines that have a pinpoint mode use an audio clue to help you understand the exact location of your potential treasure. As the center of the coil gets closer to the target, the audio response will be louder. As the coil passes the potential treasure and moves away, the audio response gets quieter.

The Art of Pinpointing

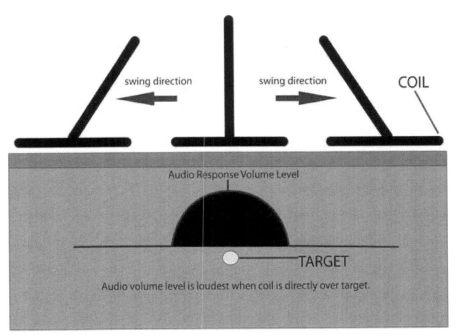

There are even some models where the pitch of the audio response will change in relation to the location of your target. The pitch and the volume will generally get higher as you get closer to your target. This image should help explain audio pinpointing a little better.

Visual Pinpointing
Some metal detectors also have a visual indicator that can help you locate the exact location of your target. Combine this visual indicator with a good audio indicator and you will have no problems pinpointing your target.

What If My Metal Detector Does Not Have A Pinpoint

Mode?

There are some metal detectors that do not have a pinpoint mode, and there are some people who just don't think that a pinpoint mode works. You don't always have to rely on a specific pinpoint mode to locate your target. There are a few proven pinpointing methods that work just as good. All of these methods vary just slightly.

The PLUS Pinpointing Method

This pinpointing method is pretty easy to master. Use your coil to identify a target by moving the coil from left to right. Once you have located the strongest audio signal, change directions with your coil by moving it front to back.

Pay close attention to the audio signal as you move your coil away from you. If the sound gets stronger, then you are moving your coil closer to the target. If the audio signal gets weaker, then you are moving your coil away from the target. The same goes for bringing your coil closer to you. These illustrations should help clear things up.

The Art of Pinpointing

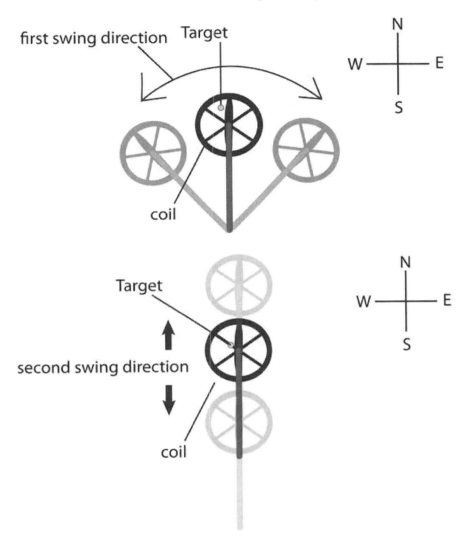

The X or 90 Degree Pinpointing Method

As you will see, this pinpointing method is very similar to the Plus method. When you locate your target, you start the pinpointing process until you hear the strongest audio signal. When you locate the strongest audio signal, you keep your coil on the area where the audio signal was the strongest and move 90 degrees in either direction.

Once you have moved 90 degrees, you start sweeping your coil. You are essentially creating an X in the ground with your swings and your target should be directly in the middle of the X. Here are a few illustrations to help visualize the concept.

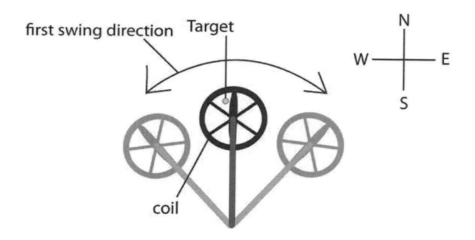

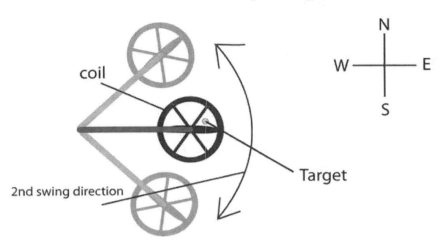

Wiggle Back Method

Yes there is yet another pinpointing method and it works very well. Locate your target and determine where the strongest audio signal is swinging left to right. Once you have located the strongest audio signal, slowly wiggle your coil backwards towards your feet. As soon as the audio signal drops away you are done. Your target should be directly in front of your coil. Here are a few illustrations to help visualize the concept.

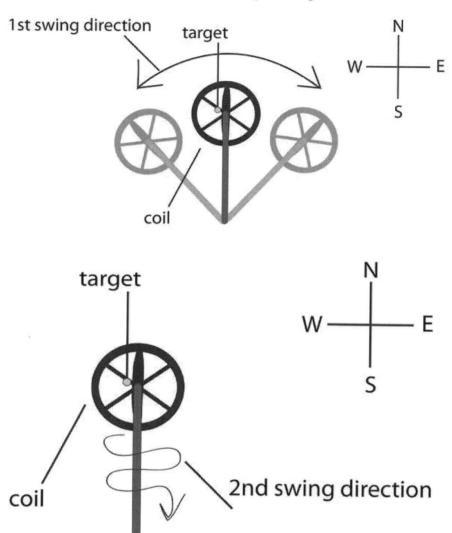

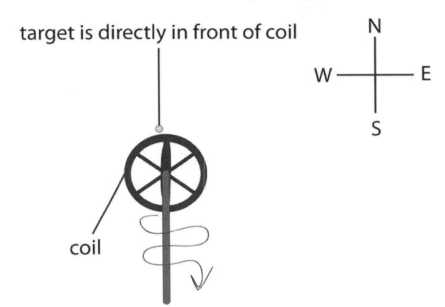

I like to mark the location of my target after I have pinpointed it. I usually just make a small depression in the ground using my finger. I have seen other people use golf ball markers or golf tees to mark the suspected location of their target. Do what works best for you.

Pinpointing is one of the most important things you can learn. I suggest practicing in your own yard to see which method works best for you and your machine.

Weak Signals

Sooner or later you are going to encounter a signal that you question. It doesn't quite sound like the rest, and you may not even be able to get it to repeat. If you are using a metal detector with some type of visual display, then your questionable signal may even appear a little erratic on the screen.

You will wind up asking yourself this question. Should I dig it? Consider the alternative. What happens if you decide not to dig it and it is a piece of gold? I always say dig it. Even if you have been hunting for hours and your arms feel like they are about to fall off. You never know what you may be passing up.

That weak signal will haunt you for a while if you choose to ignore it. Trust me on this one. I have been there, but there is a method that you can use to help you possibly strengthen that questionable signal. It is the same idea behind using the X pinpoint method.

Sometimes all you need to do is move 90 degrees in either direction and check your questionable target again. You may find that your questionable target is much stronger when you swing your coil from another direction.

This simple method does not always make the target stronger. You may find that you need to completely circle the target until you find the strongest signal. You may also never find a stronger signal. Here are a few illustrations to help visualize the concept.

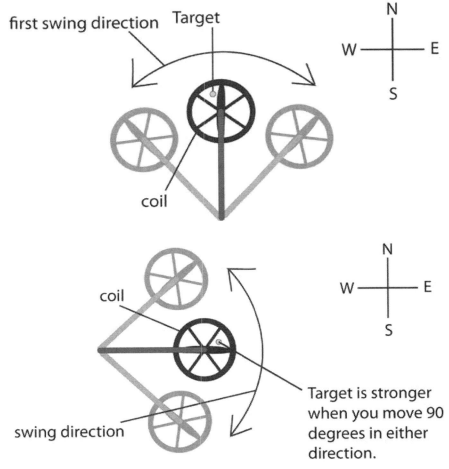

first swing direction   Target

coil

N
W —— E
S

coil

swing direction

Target is stronger when you move 90 degrees in either direction.

N
W —— E
S

If this fails to strengthen the signal, try temporarily cranking up the sensitivity on your metal detector to see if it strengthens the signal.

Recovery

The moment has arrived. You have located and pinpointed your target. It is time to uncover a piece of history that has not seen light for hundreds of years. Your treasure is almost in your hands. This is the exciting part. This is what every person who metal detects lives for, the recovery.

How are you going to get your treasure out of the earth? It is time to learn the art of recovery. Yep, just like pinpointing, recovery is an art form. It is time to get your hands dirty unless of course you are wearing gloves.

Be Careful!

First things first. Always be very careful when you are recovering your targets. You never know what you may be digging up. Your treasure could be some live ammo or even an old bomb. I am being serious here. There have been people who have recovered loaded weapons and live grenades using their metal detector.

Taking extra care will also ensure that you don't damage your buried treasure. Who knows, it could be a one of a kind gold coin. The last thing you want to do is put a big dent or a scratch in it because you were too excited to take things nice and easy.

Different Recovery Methods

There is more than one way to get that treasure out of the ground, and choosing the right recovery method really depends on the location you are hunting. There are some places where you can dig huge holes making the place look like a war zone, and there are other places where you can't disturb a single blade of grass.

If you are hunting out in the middle of the woods, then you can dig big holes as deep as you want. Just make sure you fill them in when you are done.

The same goes for the beach. Dig as much and as deep as you want. Kids will gather around you wondering what you are doing, and when you tell them you are hunting treasure, they will want to help you dig.

Recovery

There are specially designed relic shovels for digging through tough root infested ground you will find in the woods, and there are beach scoops that make it really simple to get your treasure out of the beach sand. My dad always said, "Use the right tool for the job." This is especially true when it comes to recovering your treasure while metal detecting.

There are some places where you have to be very careful how you recover your targets. Any place that has a well manicured lawn is the perfect example, and well manicured lawns are always loaded with treasure. In order to recover your targets here, you will need to learn how to cut a plug or use a probe. Can you guess what the next chapter is going to be about?

Cutting A Perfect Plug

This is the most commonly used method to recover a target. It lets you recover the target without doing any damage to the ground. With a little bit of practice, no one will even be able to tell you were there.

This is where a good handheld recovery tool comes in handy. It will help you cut through the ground like a hot knife through butter. Yes I did just use that age old cliché. Sorry, but it is the perfect example.

There are a few things that will make your job of cutting a perfect plug nothing but a nightmare. Roots will make it almost impossible to cut a good plug, and you can forget about cutting a good plug in extremely dry soil conditions.

Other than these two scenarios, learning how to cut a good plug is simple. Are you ready for the highly informative and highly skilled illustrations? Who am I kidding? My 8 year old daughter draws better than I do.

There are two basic ways to cut a plug. You can decide which one works best for you. There are also slight variations to each plug cutting style. Again, it is up to you to figure out which way works best for you and the current soil conditions.

Circular Plug With Hinge

Cutting A Perfect Plug

This is one of the more common methods for cutting a plug. Insert your hand held digging tool into the ground a few inches behind your target. You can then use a sawing like action and move your digging tool to the right or the left in a half circle pattern. Using your digging tool like a saw only works with a digging tool that has a serrated edge and if the soil is very soft.

If the soil is packed harder, you can use a different method that works well. You will have to remove your digging tool from the ground and reinsert it every few inches until you have cut a half circle like the image below.

Once you have cut your half circle, use your digging tool to gently lift the plug from the ground by sticking your digging tool back into the ground along the area you already cut. Gently push the handle of your digging down while gently lifting at the same time like the image below.

The plug should lift along the area you cut and fold up on the hinged side you did not cut like the images below.

Cutting A Perfect Plug

This method works great for shallow targets. Once you have the plug up and out of the way, you can use your metal detector or better yet your pinpointer to locate the target in the plug or the earth below it. (The next chapter covers using a pinpointer or your metal detector to locate your target in the plug or the soil below it.)

The hinged plug method works good because it allows you to fold the plug right back into the ground where it came from like the image below. Just gently push the plug back into the ground. It will look like you were never even there!

Circle Plug With No Hinge

Cutting a circle plug with a hinge is great for shallow targets, but what works best when you have to retrieve something a little deeper? That is when you cut a plug without a hinge.

This way you can move the entire plug out of the way and remove even more soil from below the plug. The same concept applies. Look at the images below.

Use your digging tool to cut a complete circle this time like the image above.

Just like before, use your digging tool to gently pry the plug up by pushing down on the handle. Your plug should pop right out the ground like the image below.

Now you should have easy access to the ground below the plug. Time to pluck that piece of treasure from the ground.

Lay a towel or a shirt down on the ground next to your hole like the image below.

Cutting A Perfect Plug

Why do this? When you start digging, you are going to need a place to store all of the dirt. Putting it on a towel or in this case a shirt, allows you to easily put the dirt right back in the hole. If you don't do this, you will never be able to get all the dirt back in the hole. It will leave a mess. Just place all the dirt you remove from the hole on the shirt just like the image below.

Cutting A Perfect Plug

Once you have used your pinpointer or your metal detector to help you locate your target, use the shirt or towel to put all of the dirt back in the hole. Gently pat it down with your hands, and place the plug back on top. When you are done, the area should look like the image below. There should be no sign that you were ever there.

The Square or Rectangular Plug

Some people prefer to cut a square or rectangular shaped plug. A square plug will be even easier to put back in the ground and leave no sign that you were ever there. Look at these images below. With the circular plug, you can see where the plug was cut if you look hard, but you can't see anything where the square plug was cut.

You can't see any plug cut marks where the square plug was!

Adjusting the Angle of Your Digging Tool

You can use your digging tool to adjust the size and diameter of the plug. If you insert your digging tool into the ground at an angle, you can cut a cone shaped plug. Inserting your digging tool straight into the ground makes a wider plug. Look at the illustrations below.

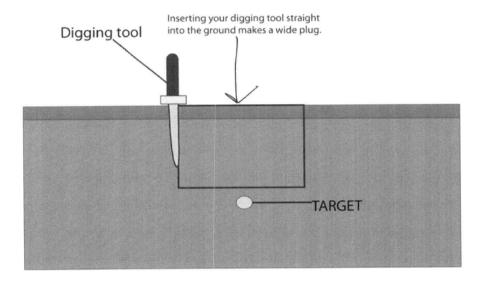

Digging tool

Inserting your digging tool straight into the ground makes a wide plug.

TARGET

Cutting A Perfect Plug

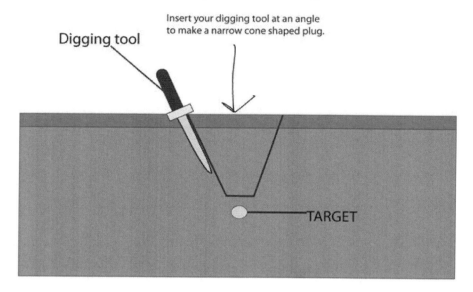

Practice makes perfect. Use these tips and methods to help you master the art of cutting a perfect plug. Pretty soon you will be a plug cutting expert.

Using A Probe

Remember how I said cutting a plug in dry soil conditions is next to impossible? That is where using a probe will make it easier to recover your target. This method works well when your target is less than 5 inches deep, and it takes some serious practice to get it down.

First, you need a probe. This is a small hand held tool that looks much like a flat head screwdriver but with a much duller tip. In fact, it is a good idea to use a probe that is not made from metal. Just imagine what a sharp metal tip would do to the surface of a 100 year old coin.

A small wooden dowel works nice, or an old fishing rod works well too. There are even some people who have made their own custom probes from old ice picks or screwdrivers. Using a probe will cause the least amount of damage to the ground.

In order to use this tool, you will have to pinpoint your target's location exactly. Once you have pinpointed your target, use the probe to locate the target and the depth. Slowly slide the probe into the soil until you feel it come into contact with the target like the image below.

Using A Probe

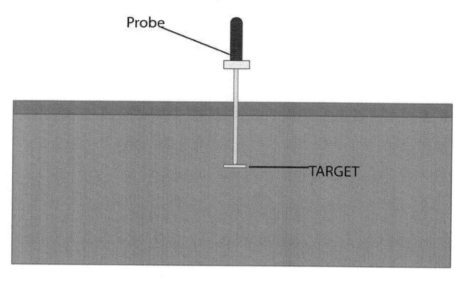

Using A Probe

Using your finger, note the depth of the target on the shaft of the probe.

Lift the probe just slightly away from the target and rotate the probe in a small circle like the image below. Rotating the probe should loosen up the soil and open a small hole in the ground above the target.

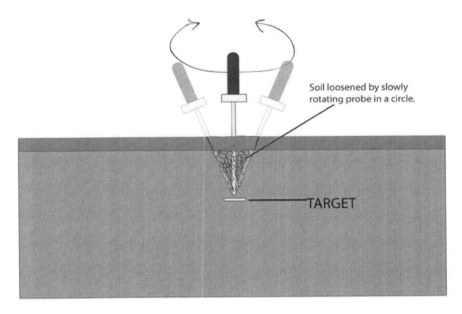

Soil loosened by slowly rotating probe in a circle.

TARGET

Now its time for the fun part. Its time to get that target out of the ground. Insert your probe at an angle underneath the target and gently lift it out of the ground like the images below.

Using A Probe

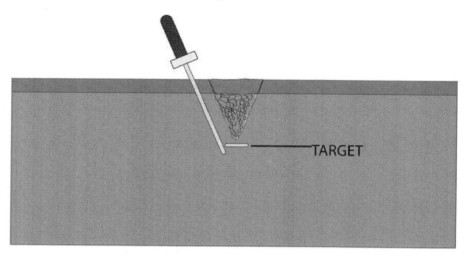

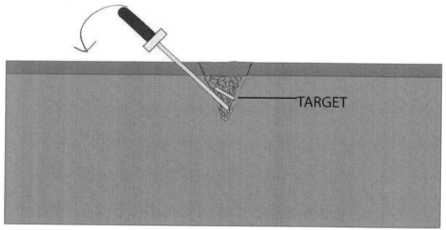

Using A Probe

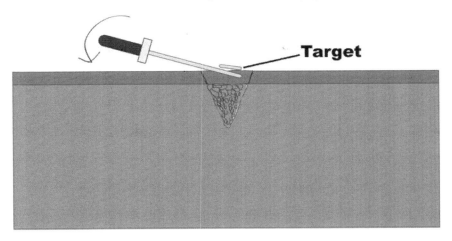

Once you have removed the target from the ground, push any dirt that came out with it back into the small hole in the ground and gently push the grass back in place. Once you are done, it should look like you were never even there.

This method can be very difficult if the target is a coin on its side. It can be even more difficult if the target is a ring, but using a probe is the best method for recovering a target when you don't want to do any damage to the ground.

Recovery Part 2

Finally, the time has come. It is time to get that piece of treasure. (I know, I know. I keep saying that, but this time I mean it.) You have pinpointed your target and you have cut a plug or dug a hole. Where is the treasure?

There are some pretty simple ways to locate your treasure. Let's take a look at using your metal detector to locate the treasure.

The first thing you should do is scan the plug with your metal detector to see if your piece of treasure is in there. Look at the image below. There is no need to get up if you are on the ground. Just wave the plug near your metal detector coil.

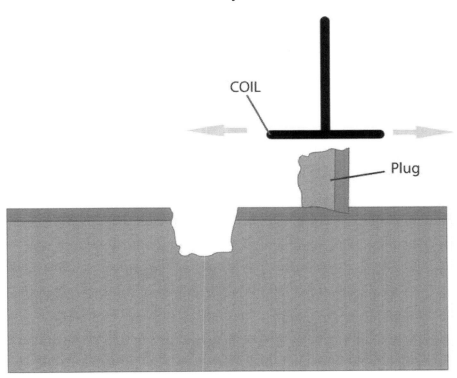

If your metal detector gives you a response on the plug, then you will need to slowly break the plug apart to locate your target. I like to cut the plug in half and then scan each half. This makes it easier to put the plug back in the ground.

If your metal detector does not give you a response on the plug, then it is time to scan the hole.

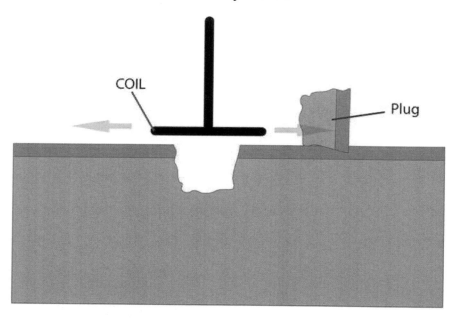

If your metal detector gives you a response on the hole, then you need to continue using your digging tool to remove small amounts of dirt from the hole. Be careful not to damage your target.

I like to loosen the dirt with my digging tool and take handfuls of the dirt and wave them in front of my metal detector coil until I have located my piece of treasure. Be mindful of any jewelry you may be wearing on the hand you are using to wave in front of the coil. If you are wearing a ring, it will most likely be seen by the metal detector.

What happens if you scan the plug and the hole and don't get a signal? Don't panic. This happens quite often. The target is still most likely in the hole and you have simply removed the halo effect that helped to amplify your target. See the images below.

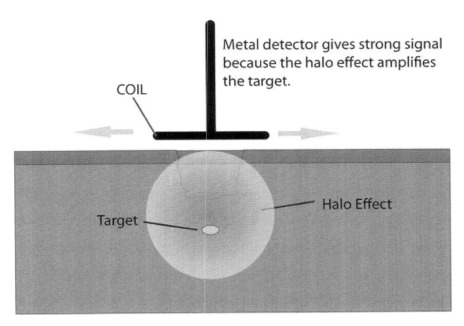

Metal detector gives strong signal because the halo effect amplifies the target.

COIL

Target

Halo Effect

Because of this, your metal detector can no longer see the target. Keep digging. There is a really good chance your target is still in that hole.

There are a few times when you may not be able to retrieve your target when this happens. If you are detecting in very soft soil conditions like mud or wet beach sand, then your target could be sinking every time you remove some earth. You may have also knocked the target on its side, or you just did not pinpoint the target accurately.

There is one trick that seems to work very well in this type of situation. If your metal detector has a pinpoint mode, it will generally still pick up the target. Try pinpoint mode before you give up.

If you can manage to get your metal detector coil in the hole, then this can help too.

In cases like this, it really pays to have a good hand held pinpointer. I strongly advise you purchase a pinpointer if you have not already done so. Let's take a closer look at a pinpointer and how it can help in a situation just like this one.

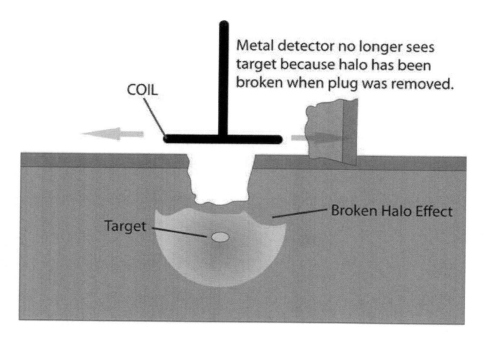

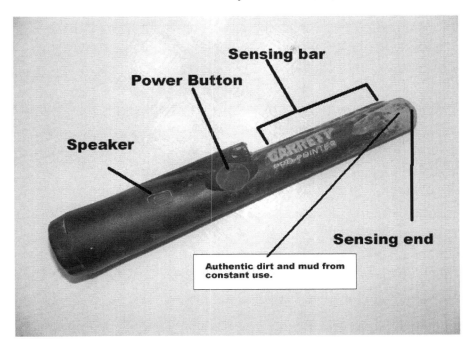

Sensing bar

Power Button

Speaker

Sensing end

Authentic dirt and mud from constant use.

This is my trusty Garrett Pro pinpointer. It is essentially a small hand held metal detector and it has made finding targets so much easier. It features two ways to help you locate your target. It has an audio indicator and the handle vibrates.

The audio indicator is a simple series of beeps that get faster as you move the pinpointer closer to your target. The vibration does the same thing. The handle will vibrate faster when the pinpointer is closer to the target. This is a great tool.

Use the pinpointer to scan the plug. If the target is not in the plug, then use the pinpointer to scan the hole. If the target is really deep in the hole, then your pinpointer may not be able to detect it.

Remove some earth and set it on a towel. Make sure you scan all of the dirt you removed, and then scan the hole. Your pinpointer should be able to locate your target even if you have broken the halo effect.

That's it! Congratulations! You now have your piece of treasure in your hand. You can fill the hole and move on to the next spot, but what if there was more than one target in the hole? Did you just bury it and leave it for someone else to find?

Always double and triple check your hole when you retrieve a target. Use your metal detector and your pinpointer. You may be surprised by the amount of targets you can recover in one hole. I recovered $12.00 in quarters in one hole. That is a total of 48 coins for those of you that don't know American currency denominations. I still don't know how 48 coins got in one small area, but they did. Maybe it was a small cache! Always double and even triple check your hole before you fill it in.

Now that you have your target in your hand, the two most common questions that arise will be:

- How do I clean it?

Recovery Part 2

- What the heck is it?

Most of the treasure you find will be very dirty, tarnished or encrusted. You will also find plenty of targets that you can't identify. Can you guess what the next two chapters will cover?

Identifying Your Finds

Before you can learn the right way to clean up your finds
and make them more presentable, you have got to identify
them. Identifying your finds can be really simple, or it can
be really difficult. It really depends on what you think your
find is.

If you have something and you have no earthly idea what it

could be, then joining one of the many metal detecting communities out there will give you an answer. I will talk a little more about these in a later chapter.

Many of the metal detecting communities have members that love to help people identify the things they have uncovered. I have posted several unidentifiable things to these communities myself, and there is always someone who can positively identify them. Once you know what you have, you can move on to cleaning it up, but only if that is the best choice.

Identifying Old Coins

You can use some of the metal detecting communities to help you identify older coins, or you can do a little bit of research yourself. The Internet is a great resource for this type of research.

Sometimes all you need to do is Google some of the writing that can be seen on the face of the coin. Pay particular close attention to dates and mint marks. These are often the best clues for helping you identify older coins.

This is a great method for identifying coins, but what if you can't get to the Internet?

I recommend buying a really good coin book to help you identify your coin finds. One of the best books for identifying American coins is called: **The Official Red Book**. You can find this book at just about any bookstore, and of course you can also order it on the Internet.

I always keep a copy of this book, and I love looking through it. It has helped me identify many coins, and because I have looked at this book so much, I often know what the coins are the moment I see them.

For those of you that are not in America, there are books that can help you identify just about every coin in the world. One of the most popular is called: **Standard Catalog of World Coins**. Another good book for identifying world coins is called: **The World Encyclopedia of Coins & Coin Collecting**.

Identifying Old Relics

Relics can be really difficult to identify, especially if they are made from iron and they have spent a lot of time in the ground. They may only slightly resemble their former selves.

If you did a fair amount of research on the area where you are hunting, then you should have a good idea of what you may have found, but there will be plenty of instances when you find relics that just don't belong in the area.

When this happens, I always turn to the metal detecting community for answers. No matter what it is you have found, there will always be someone who can help you positively identify your relic.

You can also use the Internet to help you identify some of your older relics, especially if they happen to be war items like Civil War bullets. There are plenty of great resources out there that document these types of relics. You can do a Google search for, "Civil War bullets" to get some excellent results.

Identifying Jewelry

There is a really good chance that some of the treasure you find will be old jewelry. It can be a thrilling experience removing a plug and seeing a glimmer of gold in the earth below. It can be an even more thrilling experience when that glimmer of gold turns out to be an old gold ring that is loaded with diamonds, rubies, emeralds or any other type of precious stone, but how can you tell what that ring is made of? How can you tell if those stones are real?

Believe it or not, identifying old jewelry is not all that hard. You will need a couple of tools to help you in the process. A good jeweler's loupe is a must for identifying jewelry. You can find them on the Internet for just a couple of dollars. A magnifying glass will work too, but not quite as good.

Almost all rings are marked along the inside of the band. Here are a few examples.

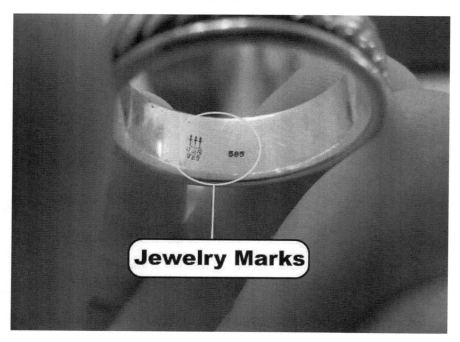

Let's take a closer look at those marks to see what they say.

This ring is unique because it is made from both silver and gold. I know this because the 925 marking means 92.5% silver and the 585 marking means 58.5% gold. I explain common ring and jewelry markings just a few paragraphs down.

Not all pieces of jewelry have clear concise markings and some are not marked at all. I will talk a little more about this a little later.

Identifying Jewelry

Use your jeweler's loupe to closely inspect the jewelry. Look over every single centimeter.

- For rings, most of the markings will be along the inside of the band.
- For necklaces, bracelets and chains, most markings are somewhere close to the clasp.
- For earrings, look around the backside of the earring.

Take note of anything you can legibly read. These markings can tell you what the jewelry is made from. They can tell you who originally made the jewelry and what the stones might be too. Here are the most common jewelry marks and what they mean.

10k – This means 10 karat gold. It can be white, yellow, or rose. About 40% gold.

10kp – There seems to be some speculation on this one, but every time I have found this, it meant 10 karat plumb, which means exactly 10 karats. About 40% gold.

14k – This means 14 karat gold. It can be white, yellow, or rose and it means that the jewelry contains 58% gold.

14kp – This means that the jewelry is pure 14 karats. About 58% gold.

18k – This means 18 karat gold. It can be white, yellow, or rose. About 75% gold.

20k – This means 20 karat gold. About 83% gold.

22k – This means 22 Karat gold. About 91% Gold

24k – This means 24 karat gold. This is 100% pure gold!

.417 – Same as 10k.

.585 – Same as 14k.

.750 – Same as 18k.

.833 – Same as 20k.

.999 – Same as 24k.

PD 950 – This means that item is made from 95% palladium.

PLAT – This means platinum.

PT – This can also mean platinum and can be prefixed, or followed by a number.

900 – This means platinum. It is 90% Platinum.

950 – This also means platinum. It is 95% Platinum.

Identifying Jewelry

Stainless Steel – These rings have gained popularity. They are usually marked: Stainless Steel, S.S., or Steel.

Silver- Self Explanatory.

S. Silver – This means Sterling Silver

Sterling Silver – Self Explanatory.

925 – This means the item is silver. About 92.5% pure.

Titanium – These rings are very light.

Tungsten – These are becoming more popular too. Most of the times they are an odd flat black color.

CZ – If you find a ring with a stone in it, this means that the stone is cubic zirconia.

CW – If you find a ring with a stone in it, this could be prefixed or followed by a number. This number would be the amount of total carat weight of the diamond.

Before you get too excited and start doing the happy dance, a ring mark does not always mean that the ring is real. There are plenty of counterfeit pieces of jewelry out there. Luckily there are ways to easily test the authenticity of a piece of jewelry or anything that may be made from a precious metal.

You can get a small acid test kit that will let you test a small portion of the item in question.

The acids are for testing different purities of metal. You will have to scratch a small portion of your jewelry on a small stone, and then place a drop of acid on the stone where you scratched the metal object. If the metal residue dissolves, your item is not real. If it does not dissolve, congratulations on your find! Here is a good example.

The acid did not dissolve the gold. That means the gold is 14kt because I used a 14kt acid test kit!

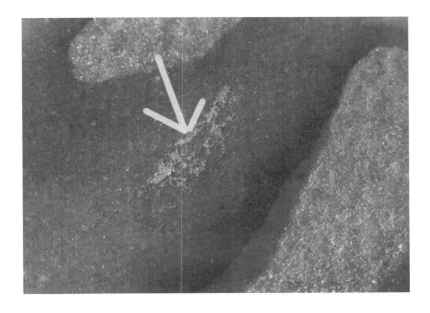

Identifying Jewelry

There are different acids for different types of metal. You can purchase an acid test kit that will help you test the purity of a variety of different metals.

What About Diamonds or Other Precious Stones?

Learning to spot a real diamond from a fake is an art form. It can take years to master this art. When you are looking at what you think may be a diamond, you are looking for small pieces of carbon. They will appear as black dots throughout the stone. A high powered jeweler's loupe will give you an up close and personal look at the suspected diamond.

A diamond with more carbon or black spots will have a smaller value. A diamond with less carbon will have a higher value. These bits of carbon affect the clarity of the stone. If you don't see any carbon, you could have an extremely valuable diamond in your hands.

There are some other signs that your precious stones may or may not be real. You will rarely find diamonds mounted in silver jewelry. I am not saying they don't exist because they do, but they are very rare.

If your piece of jewelry is gold or platinum, then there is a 99% chance that any stones in the jewelry will be real.

You have a few other choices for testing the authenticity of your newly found treasure. There are electronic diamond testers on the market that will tell you whether or not your diamond is real. They are not very expensive. If you are finding a lot of jewelry with diamonds, then you can afford to pick up a diamond tester.

Your other option is a local jeweler. Your jeweler should have no problems identifying your newly found piece of jewelry, but be careful around jewelers. I would not let them go into the back room to "get a closer look" if you think you have something that is extremely valuable. There are a lot of dishonest people out there and they will take full advantage of your lack of knowledge.

The jeweler should also be able to tell you the value of your new find. Just understand that value is always relative. Just because a jeweler states your new piece of jewelry is worth thousands does not mean someone will be willing to pay this.

You may also want to pay the jeweler to give your new piece of jewelry a good professional cleaning, or you could use some of the cleaning methods in the next chapter.

There are two rules that you should live by when you are trying to identify your finds. Never assume anything, and never throw anything away until it has been positively identified. You never know what you may have.

Cleaning Your Finds

To clean, or not to clean. That is the question! There are some situations where cleaning your finds just might destroy the value. If there is any doubt in your mind, then you probably should not be cleaning your new piece of treasure. This is especially true with old coins that have a nice natural patina. They are far more valuable in their current state than if you cleaned them. The same could be said of any old relics that you may find.

There will also be times when you will want to clean an item in order to properly display it or sell it. Here are some of the best methods for cleaning some of the great treasures you are going to be finding. Let's start with coins.

Cleaning Clad Coins

Over a period of time, you will wind up with a lot of clad coins. You may even want to take them all to the bank and deposit them. Cleaning clad is fairly easy because you don't have to worry about doing any damage to these coins. Their only monetary value is their current face value.

A rock tumbler is an excellent way to give these types of coins a good cleaning. If you don't have a rock tumbler, then there are a few other great ways to clean the mountain of clad coins you have been finding.

Cleaning Clad Coins

I use an old plastic fruit juice jug. I put some sand, and a mixture of vinegar and water in the juice jug along with all the coins and give it a good shaking. Then I empty all the coins into an old colander and rinse them with fresh water. This is usually good enough for the bank.

Cleaning Valuable Coins

The value of older coins is based on a few things. The amount of like coins that were minted, and the current condition of the coin. If you happen to damage the coin while you attempt to clean it, then you could be making a huge mistake.

If you have an older coin that you want cleaned, then you had better leave this up to the professionals. There are professional coin cleaning and grading services out there. The two most popular are:

Numismatic Conservation Service
http://www.ncscoin.com/
Phone: 941.360.3996
email: Service@NCScoin.com

PCGS or Professional Coin Grading Service
http://www.pcgs.com/
United States toll free phone number: 800-447-8848
Outside of the United States phone number: 949-833-0600
Email: info@pcgs.com

If you have an older coin that is not extremely valuable and you want to clean it up yourself, there are a few proven methods that work quite well.

The Slow Coin Cleaning Method

If you don't mind waiting a little while (sometimes 2-3 months), then soak your coin in olive oil. This method has proven to clean even the most stubborn dirty coin with no visible damage. The down side is that this method can take a very long time. If you can wait, stick to this method. If you can't wait, then try some of these other great cleaning methods.

Faster Coin Cleaning Options

Toothpaste works wonders on old tarnished metals. Work a small dab of toothpaste onto the surface of the coin using your fingers. You can also use a soft bristled toothbrush to help loosen up some of the crud on the coin. Rinse and repeat until the coin looks good.

Another neat trick involves a little bit of science. Rub the old coin with a wet piece of tinfoil. This creates a mild electrolysis effect and cleans the surface of the coin. You can also go the full electrolysis route if you want. I will explain that cleaning method in a little bit.

Some people have also had great results cleaning coins using baking soda, vinegar and lemon juice. They can all be used separately, or in some type of crazy mad scientist concoction. Just be careful if you plan on mixing chemicals. You could be asking for all sorts of problems.

Cleaning Jewelry

A jeweler will always be able to make an old piece of jewelry shine just like new, but there are a few tricks that you can try first. My wife is a pro at using nothing but toothpaste on any old jewelry that I bring home, and she makes it look as good as new.

She just rubs toothpaste into the surface of the jewelry. Sometimes she will use a soft cloth to polish the item in question with the toothpaste. She then rinses and repeats until the jewelry is nice and sparkly.

This works well with pretty much any type of metal that jewelry is made from, except junk jewelry. Junk jewelry gets so tarnished and dirty because it is junk. There is very little you can do to this type of jewelry that will make it look even remotely good.

Cleaning Precious Stones

Precious stones, especially diamonds tend to get a little dirty over time. The oils and greases from our skin stick to the surface of precious stones and cause all sorts of problems that make the stone look less desirable. Cleaning the stones will not only restore their natural luster, but it will also make them more presentable.

There are a few things to consider before you start attacking your precious stones. You are responsible for any damage that you may do. You could also easily knock the stone or stones out of the piece of jewelry. They could fall into the sink and your great piece of treasure is now lost again. If you have any doubts about cleaning jewelry with stones, leave this job to a professional. If you want to tackle this job at home, then here is what you need to do.

The first ingredient is warm water. The warm water will help break up any oil or grease that may have accumulated on the surface of the stone, but warm water is not enough to make precious stones glitter and sparkle.

You can use a small amount of Ivory brand dish soap, liquid jewelry cleaner or a drop or two of ammonia mixed in the water. This combination helps remove all the gunk that may have built up on the surface and the underside of your newly acquired precious stones.

I bet you never thought you would become an expert coin cleaner and an expert jewelry cleaner when you thought about metal detecting, did you? It is all part of the greatest hobby in the world.

Cleaning Relics

Determining the best way to clean relics really depends on what the relic is made from. In some cases, you may not want to clean the relic. It may be more valuable in its current state. I know I keep saying this, but it is very important to remember this.

For those of you who are determined to clean up those old rusty relics, then it is time to step into a somewhat dangerous area. First things first. We are going to be talking about electricity and water. These two things don't play nicely together. One mistake could give you the shock of a lifetime. It could also kill you. I take no liability for the problems you create by using this method to clean coins, jewelry or relics. You have been warned. You are proceeding at your own risk. Let's talk electrolysis.

Electrolysis

Using electrolysis is one of the best ways to clean just about anything made from metal, but not everyone has an electrolysis setup in their garage. If you do happen to have a homemade electrolysis setup in your garage, then you are lucky. You can skip over this entire chapter.

The great thing about this method is its simplicity. It is very easy to setup and even easier to use. There are also several different variations to this setup.

There are electrolysis setups that have more power. These setups are excellent at removing rust from larger iron relics. There are also smaller less powerful setups that are great at cleaning coins.

Before we dive into creating an electrolysis setup. Let's have a closer look at the dangers involved.

Danger # 1 – Water and electricity don't mix. I have already said this. You can get shocked if you don't pay attention to what you are doing.

Danger # 2 – Your electrolysis setup will create toxic waste if you are using stainless steel in your electrolysis setup.

Danger # 3 – The electrolysis process creates gas. The gas that is created is hydrogen. While the amount of hydrogen being produced is very small, it is still extremely flammable. Do not place your electrolysis setup next to any open flames. Pilot lights, lighters or candles. You get the picture. Build your electrolysis unit outside or in a well ventilated area.

Electrolysis

Now that you are aware of the dangers, let's look over the supplies. You will need the following:

- Eye protection. You only get one set of eyes. Protect them.
- Gloves.
- Large non-conductive plastic container. A plastic bucket or a plastic storage container should work just fine.
- Automotive battery charger or an AC/DC (rock on!) power supply.
- A flat piece of iron or steel. Rebar works great, or an old kitchen pan. Stainless steel will create some toxic waste.
- Washing soda, baking soda or salt. Washing soda is not baking soda and it works best. It is made by Arm & Hammer, and it can be found in smaller stores or online.
- A measuring spoon of some sort.
- Water

That's it. Let's build this thing. This diagram explains everything clearly. Look it over first.

Electrolysis

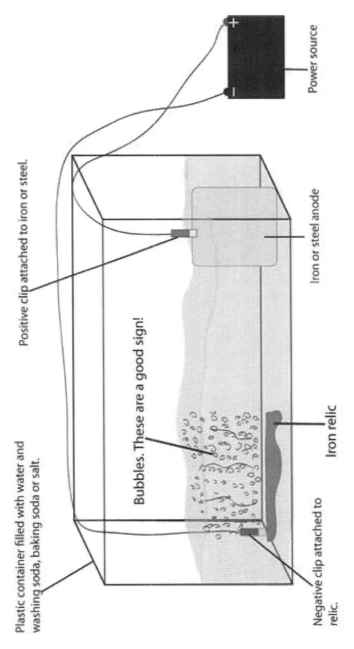

Power source

Positive clip attached to iron or steel.

Iron or steel anode

Bubbles. These are a good sign!

Plastic container filled with water and washing soda, baking soda or salt.

Iron relic

Negative clip attached to relic.

Electrolysis

Put on your gloves and safety glasses. You need to clean the dirty piece of treasure first. A wire brush and some mild soap and water are perfect for cleaning the item in question before you start the electrolysis process.

Take your plastic container and fill it with enough water to completely submerge the piece of metal you want to clean. The plastic container has to be made from non-conductive material.

Now it is time to add the washing soda, baking soda or salt to the water. Remember, washing soda and baking soda are two very different things. Washing soda works the best. Add one tablespoon per gallon of water and stir it up. You now have an electrolyte solution.

Connect the negative lead from your power source to your rusty iron relic and submerge it in the water. Connect the positive lead to your flat piece of steel and submerge it in the solution as well.

Make sure the relic and the anode (flat piece of steel) are not touching. In fact, keep them as far away from each other as possible. Take a look at that image again. See how far away the two items are?

If you are using alligator clips attached to your negative and positive leads, make sure you keep the positive lead out of the water. It will make it last longer. The item that is attached to the positive lead will eventually disintegrate. If

you submerge your positive alligator clip, it will
disintegrate over a period of time as well.

Once everything is submerged and attached, it is time to
plug in your power source and turn it on. You still there?
Okay good. You didn't blow anything up. If everything is
working properly, you should see some bubbles coming
from your rusty old relic.

How Long Do You Keep It Submerged?
This depends on quite a few things. It depends on the
amount of power you have powering your electrolysis
setup and the size of the anode. Your best bet is to just
keep a close eye on it. If you leave it submerged for too
long, you could damage the item being cleaned.

What Happens Next?
The water in your electrolysis setup will start to get dark
and dirty. If your item was really rusty, you may even see a
thick brown foam forming on the surface of the water. This
is good, but don't go sticking your hands in the water. You
must shut down the power first.

Shut Off the Power to Your Electrolysis Setup
Once you have unplugged your power source, you are
ready to reach in there and see what the electrolysis
process has revealed. If everything worked right, your
piece of treasure should be pretty good and clean now. The
next step is drying your newly cleaned piece of treasure
before the rust can take over again.

Drying the Relic

There are a few ways to do this. Be careful not to burn yourself. You could use a hairdryer to dry the iron relic, an infrared heat lamp, or a conventional oven.

Preserving Relics

Once the relic is completely dry, it is time to preserve and prevent the rust from taking over again. Some people use a clear coat of spray paint, but this can have adverse effects. It can also cause even more rusting in the future if done incorrectly.

The best proven methods for preserving these types of relics use wax. There are a couple of wax preserving methods that work really well. You can use car wax as long as it does not have any type of abrasive material in it. Briwax works great. It helps to seal the relic and prevent moisture damage.

You will have to apply several coats and buff the relic between each coat. If done correctly, you should have a nice protective barrier that will last for years to come.

The other method involves quite a bit more work. You have to use Microcrystalline Wax. If you intend to use this method of preservation, then you will not have to dry the iron relic.

Submerge the relic into a heated vat of Microcrystalline

wax. The perfect temperature is right around 175 degrees Fahrenheit (79 degrees Celsius). The iron relic must stay submerged until no more bubbles emerge from the vat of hot wax.

Once this happens, the wax is then cooled and the iron relic is removed and any residual wax is removed immediately. This method produces a long lasting barrier that will not yellow and it will prevent any future rust.

Selling Your Finds

At one point or another, you may want to actually sell some of that treasure you have found. If you have a lot of gold, you may want to hold on to it. It will only increase in value, but if you have to part with some of your treasure there are some right ways and some wrong ways to go about doing it.

First things first. Stay away from pawn shops. No offense to any pawn shop owners that may be reading this book. Pawn shops just don't pay full value on anything. If you need some cash in a hurry, then a pawn shop is your best bet. If you can wait a few days, then you can get twice or even three times what a pawn shop offers you.

Is it okay to sell your finds? This is up to you. You may feel morally obligated to find the original owner of an item that you have found. There is nothing wrong with this. I have returned several pieces of jewelry, but I have sold quite a few too.

Selling off some of your finds is a great way to upgrade to some better equipment. A good metal detector does not come cheap, and you have worked hard for all of your treasure. There is nothing wrong with rewarding yourself.

You can sell just about any type of metal that you find. Of course you will be able to sell gold, silver and platinum, but many people forget that you can sell old lead fishing weights too. Those things are not cheap, and fisherman will gladly pay you for them. I have sold a lot of lead weights this way. Just think of it as recycling.

Selling some of your precious metals.
There are several ways to sell off some of your precious metal items. You can try to sell your treasure online through some of the popular websites, and there are plenty of people who make good money doing this, or you can sell your precious metal items to a refinery. They pay top dollar for gold, silver, platinum and other precious metals.

Some people won't use refineries because it involves sending all of your valuable precious metals through the mail. There is a good chance that your package full of gold will magically disappear. There is an easy way to avoid this. Never send it all in one batch. Plus, the US postal service offers insurance and signed proof of delivery. You make the call.

Selling Your Finds

I have sold a lot of gold this way, and I have never had a problem. You simply securely send your gold, silver or platinum to the refinery and a week or two later you get a nice check in the mail.

I have used two refineries with no problems. Here is their contact information.

ARA
http://www.aragold.com/
1-800-216-9796
972-620-6020
2431 Walnut Ridge St.
Dallas, TX 75229

Midwest Refineries
1-800-356-2955
4471 Forest Ave.
Waterford, Michigan 48328

You may even be able to sell your treasure to a local jeweler that you have an arrangement with. This is a great way to get top dollar. Just make sure that the jeweler is someone you can trust.

Time to get that new metal detector that you have had your eyes on for months. This is one great thing about metal detecting. It is the only hobby that really does pay for itself.

Join the Community

Just like you, there are plenty of other people out there that have the desire to dig up old treasure. Luckily, there are plenty of places where all of us can get together and exchange stories, tips and other metal detecting related stuff.

If you want to reach out and connect with other people, then the best place to start is with a local metal detecting club. There are metal detecting clubs in every state in the United States. If you are not from the United States, then you still may even be able to find a local club in your area using this method. Head over to the Internet and search for the biggest city closest to you along with the words metal detecting club.

For instance: if you live in Orlando, search for "Orlando metal detecting club" without the quotes. Almost every metal detecting club has some sort of website.

Metal detecting clubs are a great way to find hunting partners, learn about the hobby and see some of the great stuff people are finding. Metal detecting clubs will often plan group hunts as well. It can be great to get together with other people who enjoy the hobby as much as you do. You will get the opportunity to meet some older people who have been hunting for treasure for their entire life.

Join the Community

Online Communities

If you can't seem to find a local club, then you are still in luck. There are several great online metal detecting communities out there where thousands of eager metal detecting enthusiasts meet every single day from all over the world to share their finds, tips and advice.

The amount of information that can be found and learned from these online communities is invaluable, and you don't even have to take part in any of the online conversations if you don't feel like it. You can sit on the sidelines and watch and read everything quietly.

These online communities also have sections devoted to helping you identify those pieces of treasure that you can't seem to identify on your own. Don't be afraid to reach out and ask for help. Almost everyone in the online metal detecting community will be more than eager to help you.

I do have a word of warning though. If you have found something that is rare or extremely valuable, be cautious about posting it online. There are some people who browse these forums looking for an easy way to steal a person's secret spots. These people are clever and they will stop at nothing to go right behind your back and hunt out an area you are trying to keep secret.

There was a time when I posted pictures of great treasures that I was finding along my local beach. It was not long until I noticed more and more people at my local beach with their metal detectors. I even noticed a couple of guys started following me.

Now don't take this the wrong way. There are far more people who are part of these online communities who are good people, and I have met and made some great friends using these online communities, but there are always a few bad apples in the bunch. Just be careful.

Here are the top communities worth checking out.

http://www.treasurenet.com/
This is arguably the largest online treasure related community.

http://www.findmall.com/
Another excellent online community full of tips and knowledgeable people who love to help.

http://www.justgodetecting.com/

http://metaldetectingforum.com/

Thanks!

Metal detecting is a life long learning experience. You will find that you learn something new pretty much every single time you go out and hunt. If you enjoyed Metal Detecting: A Beginner's Guide, then feel free to leave a review! I would really appreciate it.

If you want to learn what it is like to metal detect at the beach and uncover loads of treasure, take a look at my best selling book entitled:

Metal Detecting the Beach

It is packed full of great beach hunting tips, tricks and secrets. It is available in digital format and paperback.

The greatest tip that I can leave you with is this. Persistence pays. You never know when you will find that next great piece of treasure. Believe me, it is out there and it is waiting for you to discover it! Get out there and have fun.

I am currently in the process of writing several more great treasure hunting books. If you want to be the first to find out about any new books that I publish, sign up to my **new book release** email list.

I promise not to share your email address with anyone, and

Thanks!

I won't send you tons of junk mail. (I will only contact you when a new book is out.)

http://eepurl.com/EyhF1

All of this information can and will help you increase your treasure pile much faster, but the only real way you are going to find some treasure is by getting out there and doing it!

Drop me a line and let me know how you are doing out there. I always love hearing about things that other people are finding. You can email me at: wordsaremything@gmail.com

Happy hunting,
Mark Smith

Made in the USA
San Bernardino, CA
11 June 2014